RADICAL NURSES
28 Stories of Resistance, Reform & Revolution

by

Mary Ellen Biggerstaff

Bildung Press   Olympia, WA

9798218452346

Printed in United States of America

First Edition

Cover, From L to R: Harriet Tubman, Emma Goldman, Waltl Whitman, Sophia Duleep Singh, Sojourner Truth, and Lillian Wald

Cover Design: Eleanor Steinhagen

Introduction

The idea for this book was sparked several years ago on June 27th, when I read that not only did Emma Goldman and I share the same birthday, but we shared the same profession, nursing. Delving into her autobiography and writings ignited a quest to uncover other extraordinary but rarely told stories. In nursing history, radicalism is a seldom-explored territory.

Icons of professional nursing such as Florence Nightingale and Mary Breckenridge are well known, but came from rigid, elite and hierarchical traditions. The legacy of 'The Angel at the Bedside', represents just a piece of nursing's rich history, but dominates the story of nursing we present in the world and teach in our schools. How many more hidden narratives of nursing activism lay dormant? How many individuals' lives wove caregiving with activism and creativity? What about those nurses who sought to dismantle hierarchies and challenged inequality?

Asking these questions took me on a five-year journey to identify and collect these stories. It also required me to think about what it meant to be a radical and what it means to be a nurse. In a statement attributed to Marx, to be radical is to grasp things at their root. Saul Alinsky states it is a belief in the common good above personal gain, a commitment to fundamental change rather than incremental reform. Radicals are vocal critics of societal norms, advocating for comprehensive solutions to systemic issues, often at great personal sacrifice.

For these stories, I use the definition of a nurse that extends beyond formal education and training, including nurses throughout history and from many traditions. Nursing history does not begin and end with professionalization in the nineteenth century, but is the act of providing care for individuals, families, and communities. It encompasses both formal and informal caregiving practices and includes roles such as religious healers, midwives, and social reformers.

Radicalism and nursing intersect uniquely in each of this book's stories. For some of the nurses, radicalism permeated both their professional and personal lives; for others, it emerged in specific contexts. These are the stories of individuals who dared to challenge conventions— sometimes through their nursing work, but often in ways that transcended the profession entirely. Beyond the physical and emotional labor traditionally associated with nursing, these stories illuminate the intellectual and transformative contributions of nurses.

The intimacy of nursing care has unique radical potential. To care for another person is to bear witness to their humanity, to reach across boundaries of social and economic class, and to build solidarity through shared vulnerability. In these moments of connection, nursing can become more than a job; it becomes an act of resistance against dehumanization and a way to stand in solidarity with the marginalized in the world. Proximity to human struggle can be an education in injustice and the means to address it. Nursing can also be a practical way of making a living while engaging in activism. The variety of these nurses' lives shows options for all of us to engage in radical acts. While some of these nurses were incredibly courageous and heroic, others were simply trying to do the right thing as they navigated the challenges of their times.

Drawing on the work of historians and biographers, this collection of biographical sketches reveals that radicalism is not an abstract concept but can be lived. These stories demonstrate how nursing has served as a platform for confronting injustice, advocating for change, and addressing the root causes of inequality.

This book is both a collection of brief biographies and a history of nurses who challenged the conventions of their time. These accounts, both inspiring and intellectually engaging, illustrate how nursing extends beyond the confines of a profession to become a force for transformation. At their core, these narratives demonstrate how acts of courage and human connection can sustain the vision of a more equitable and humane world.

These stories honor the legacy of these pioneering nurses but also invite readers to reconsider their own potential to influence meaningful change. By sharing these narratives with students, colleagues, and readers, I aim to highlight the radical potential within nursing—a potential to challenge inequities, bridge divides, and create lasting change. I hope these accounts spark in you the same sense of discovery and possibility they have inspired in me, encouraging us to broaden our perspectives, deepen our commitments, and reimagine what is possible in our lives.

Table of Contents

1. Hildegard Von Bingen   14

    A medieval German abbess who wrote on philosophy, health, science, mysticism, and composed music in addition to the practical work of providing care for her fellow sisters.

2. Juana Inés de la Cruz   17

    A writer, scholar, musician, and nun in 17th Century colonial Mexico, Sor Juana advocated for women's education and provided nursing care to the nuns in her Mexico City convent.

3. Sojourner Truth   21

    An African American abolitionist and itinerant evangelical preacher, Sojourner worked as a nurse and hospital organizer for the Freedmen's Bureau, the agency that worked to provide services to the formerly enslaved during post-Civil War Reconstruction.

4. Mary Seacole   26

    A Jamaican nurse/doctoress, Mary combined traditional Jamaican and Western medicine, building and operating hospitals in Jamaica, Panama, and Turkey during the Crimean War. She went on to write about her adventurous life and was honored by the British Empire.

5. Margaret Fuller   30

Brilliant writer, journalist, intellectual and early American feminist, she was serving as the first female correspondent during the Italian Revolution when she helped operate and run a hospital in Rome.

6. Biddy Mason   34

Born enslaved and trained as a traditional nurse and midwife, Biddy won her freedom as one of the earliest African American settlers in Los Angeles, then used her training to build a real estate philanthropy empire in L.A.

7. Walt Whitman   37

Great American poet and writer, he championed human liberation and spent much of the civil war as a volunteer nurse caring for soldiers.

8. Harriet Tubman   41

Abolitionist who helped seventy people escape slavery through the Underground Railroad, also worked as a nurse and a spy during the Civil War.

9. Kusumoto Ine   46

A Japanese-German midwife and clinician, was the first female trained in Western health care during Japan's seclusion and delivered the child of an emperor.

10. Louisa May Alcott   49

The author of the beloved classic "Little Women", and a member of the transcendentalist movement, who also wrote about her time as a nurse during the Civil War and worked for abolition and women's rights.

11. Lavinia Dock   53

An early founder of professional nursing in the United States, Lavinia was a professor, author of early nursing textbooks, co-founder of the International Council of Nurses and an advocate for labor and women's rights.

12. Lillian Wald   56

An American nurse, author, and activist, Lillian founded public health nursing as part of her work in the tenements of New York City as well as helping to support the founding of the NAACP and the suffragette movement.

13. Emma Goldman   60

Anarchist, political activist, and writer who championed freedom for all, spent years working as a midwife and nurse in New York City tenements and prisons.

14. Adah Thoms   67

A pioneering African American nurse and educator who co-founded the National Association of Colored Graduate Nurses and fought for the integration of Black nurses into the U.S. military and the American Red Cross during World War I.

15. Harriet Boyd Hawes   69

A rare female archeologist, Harriet led excavations of Minoan palaces and volunteered as a nurse in both the Greco-Turkish war and a nurse/organizer during the First World War.

16. Sophia Duleep Singh   74

The exiled granddaughter of the leader of the Sikh Empire, Sophia grew up in England as a ward of Queen Victoria and supporter of women's suffrage and for the rights of Indians in England, she worked as a volunteer nurse for Indian Soldiers in World War I.

17. Elena Arizmendi Mejía   79

Co-founder of the White Cross to provide medical care to revolutionaries in the Mexican Revolution, went on to inspire one of the most famous characters in Mexican literature, and helped pioneer the Hispanic women's movement

18. Nella Larsen   83

Author Nella Larsen was a star of Harlem Literary Renaissance, a nurse and an activist-librarian in the New York Public Library System.

19. Vera Brittain   89

A British nurse, writer, feminist and pacifist who became a bestselling author for her novel about her experience as a nurse in World War I. As a pacifist activist she fought against colonialism, apartheid, and nuclear proliferation.

20. Susie Walking Bear Yellowtail   93

A member of the Crow nation and one of the first Native American Registered Nurses, Susie worked as a nurse and outspoken advocate for her people, helping publicize the poor treatment and mass sterilization of Native women. She later went on to serve as a cultural ambassador and a national public health advisor.

21. Irena Sendler & Ala Golab-Grynburg   97

Two Polish women, one Jewish and one Catholic, trained in nursing, social work, and public health, helped lead the resistance to the Nazi extermination of the Jews in the Warsaw Ghetto, saving the lives of hundreds of children.

22. Margaret Charles Smith   103

An African American southern "granny midwife" who spent thirty years delivering babies in rural Alabama, seeing the dawn of civil rights and the crushing of the traditional midwife system by the white medical system.

23. Simone Weil   108

A French philosopher, mystic, and political activist, Simone lived her life with singular empathy and vision, and among her many works of political activism, envisioned a nurse corps to combat the evil of the Nazi regime during WWII.

24. Ruth Davidow   113

A nurse, activist and filmmaker, Ruth worked as a nurse in the Lincoln Brigade during the Spanish Civil War, supported Native rights in the occupation of Alcatraz, and made over 20 activist documentary films.

25. Salaria Kea O'Riley   117

A nurse and political activist, Salaria fought for Civil Rights and was a member of the Leftist Lincoln Brigade in the Spanish Civil War.

26. Albertina Sisulu   121

One of the founders of the African National Congress, she
tirelessly fought apartheid while working as a nurse and raising
her family during her husband's imprisonment on Robbins
Island and served as a member of post-apartheid South
African parliament.

27. Marie Branch   127

African American nurse, activist, and academic, Marie helped
found the Black Panther health care clinic in Los Angeles,
traveled to Cuba and China as an activist, and wrote
groundbreaking academic papers on combating racism in
nursing and healthcare.

28. Shirley Willer   131

A proud lesbian and nurse, Shirley was an early advocate of
the American gay rights movement of the 1950s and 1960s.

"But the effect of her being on those around her was incalculably diffusive: for the growing good of the world is partly dependent on unhistoric acts; and that things are not so ill with you and me as they might have been is half owing to the number who lived faithfully a hidden life, and rest in unvisited tombs" – George Eliot

Hildegard Von Bingen

We start with a medieval abbess, Hildegard Von Bingen. Hildegard was born in the medieval Holy Roman Empire (now Germany) in 1098. At this time, nursing largely took place within religious orders and left little written history. Hildegard would go on to be one of the great geniuses of her time, a mystic, composer, religious leader, and healer.

Born the youngest of ten children to an affluent family, her early years were marked by frequent illness and frailty. Although she had no formal education, she had a brilliant mind and enormous curiosity. At the age of five, she experienced the first of a series of mystical visions that would guide her life's path. By eight, she was sent to the Benedictine monastery at Disibodenberg. This was a common practice for noble families, and as the tenth child, she may have been considered a tithe to the church.

Hildegard was placed under the guidance of Jutta of Sponheim, an anchoress who had chosen to live her life secluded within a small cell. Inside the monastery, Hildegard's day would begin at 2 am each day with matins (morning prayers) and end with vespers (evening prayers).

At fifteen, Hildegard formally accepted religious orders to become a nun, embracing the spiritual and intellectual rigor that came with it. Under the tutelage of the monk Volmar, she received a uniquely strong education. Volmar encouraged Hildegard to document her mystical visions and healing practices, an unusual chance when literacy was rare and educated monks focused on copying existing texts. Hildegard was one of the first people in medieval Europe to write about her own knowledge and experiences.

The foundation of this monastic life was the Rule of St. Benedict, written in 529, and still in use today. The rules guided day to day activities and the praying of the Opus Dei, and emphasized the care of the sick and elderly as essential virtues. Hildegard would have received training in both nursing and healing.

Upon the death of Jutta in 1136, Hildegard was elected the head of her convent. At forty-one, Hildegard had been having spiritual visions for most of her life and spent ten years recording them as her testament to Christianity. She began to share these with the public, starting with the Scivias, a 600-page illustrated manuscript. Her work received wide acclaim, and in 1147, received the approval of the Pope.

Buoyed by this recognition, Hildegard founded a new convent at Rupertsberg in 1150, transforming it into a pilgrimage site for royalty and religious leaders. Her influence continued to grow as she embarked on preaching tours across Europe and authored other books, including the Book of the Divine Works.

Hildegard's contributions to natural science were also extraordinary. Her texts Causae et Curae and Physica explored medicinal properties of plants and advocated for a balanced diet, stress reduction, and a moral life. She documented the use of 200 plants and discussed other topics like reproduction and women's health with a bold frankness.

Hildegard's writings embraced a positive view of sexual relations and women's pleasure, including a description of the female orgasm and viewed health as the body's natural state. In addition to her writing, she was composing music about her mystical experiences and was one of the first people in Europe to write down musical compositions. Her musical *Ordo Virtutum* is a cycle of 70 religious songs that continue to be performed today. She passed away on September 17, 1179, but her legacy waspreserved in a biography written by Monk Geoffrey. Hildegard's compassionate care for the sick, her holistic approach to health, and her writing align with foundational principles of nursing. She bridged the gap between the sacred and the scientific; providing a holistic vision of humanity that holds today.

Sor Juana Inés de la Cruz

For our next story, we leap five hundred years and halfway across the world to find another remarkable woman in a Catholic religious order. Juana Inés de la Cruz, born Juana Ramirez de Asbaje in 1648 in San Miguel Nepantal, Mexico, stands as one of the great intellectuals of the 17th Century - a nun, poet, writer, scholar, and nurse.

Her birth to an unmarried mother, Isabel Ramirez de Santanilla, and an unknown father marked the beginning of a life that would challenge societal and intellectual barriers. Juana was a Criola of mixed Indigenous and Spanish heritage, and fluent in Nahuatl (the Aztec/Mexica language), Spanish and Latin. This was a century after the Spanish conquest of the Mexica/Aztec empire, and the country was under the rule of a viceroy representing the Spanish king. Most of the power in the country was held by Criollo landowners and the Catholic Church.

Despite her family's limited means, Juana's grandfather, who passed away in 1656, played a crucial role in her early education, teaching her Latin and classical literature on the family's hacienda, Panoayan. Juana was sent to Mexico City to live with extended family at age eight. At sixteen, she entered the Spanish court In Mexico City as a lady in waiting for the Viceroy's wife Donna Elonaro del Carretto. There is a story that Juana disguised herself as a male student to enter university, although she was quickly discovered and had to study privately instead.

Her brilliance and charm made her a court favorite. To test her intellect the viceroy assembled forty learned men. Juana was able to answer all their questions, arguments, and objectives. She also began writing Spanish romantic poetry.

At nineteen, Juana made the surprising decision to leave the court to enter a convent. Her reasons are somewhat mysterious, although her lack of a dowry may have made it difficult for her to marry. In a letter to a bishop, Sor Juana explained: "And so I entered the religious order, knowing that life there entailed certain conditions most repugnant to my nature; but given the total antipathy I felt toward marriage, I deemed convent life the least unsuitable and the most honorable I could elect if I were to ensure my salvation...such as wishing to live alone and wishing to have no obligatory occupation to inhibit the freedom of my studies, nor the sounds of a community to intrude upon the peaceful silence of my books."

Sor Juana's first convent stay was short, and she moved to The Convent of Santa Paula of the Order of San Jeronimo, a Hieronymite community for Criolla women founded in 1586. Here she thrived intellectually, amassing a library of 4000 books in Latin, Portuguese and Italian, and scientific and musical instruments. She studied theology, mythology, science, mathematics and music.

The religious communities founded hospitals, orphanages, schools, homes for the poor, and artistic centers in Mexico City. Convent life was hierarchical with nuns at the top, and servants, orphans, and lay sisters all living together. Juana had to hide her illegitimate birth to navigate this social order. Despite vows of poverty, nuns could rent luxurious rooms and interact with society. Their day began at 6 a.m. with prayers and mass, followed by communal work, vespers, and dinner. Sor Juana spent her time reading, writing poetry and letters. As a member of the convent, she would have provided nursing care and prayers for sick people. For twenty years, from 1669 to 1690, Sor Juana wrote prolifically, earning enough money to support her family. Her poetry, plays, and writings were famous across the Spanish Empire. She was considered an expert in theology, poetry, music, and embroidery.

Her biographer, Octavio Paz, noted her unique position as a nun who openly wrote erotic and romantic poetry, including love poetry written to women like the Countess de Parcedes. Sor Juana was able to balance these roles and was careful to avoid open conflict with the Catholic church.

This freedom ended abruptly in 1690 when the Bishop of Puebla published (without her permission) Sor Juana's critique of a priest's sermon, and his own instructions that she should cease writing and devote herself to prayer. Sor Juana's reply, "Respuesta a Sor Filotea de la Cruz", defended a woman's right to an education and intellectual life. The church punished her for this disobedience, forcing her to sell her library and instruments and give the proceeds to the poor.

During a 1695 plague outbreak at the San Jeronimo convent Sor Juana nursed the sick. Nursing and medical care offered little real help in the face of infectious disease, and the women were subjected to purges, bloodletting, and prayers. nine out of ten of the nuns at the convent died in the outbreak. Her biography reported that she attended her sisters "with compassion, without rest and without fear of their proximity." Sor Juana contracted the plague and died on April 17, at 46 years old.

Her legacy was preserved through the efforts of the Vicereine and a biography written by a priest, Diego Calleja. Only a few of Sor

Juana's writings survived and published in her complete works. Sor Juana's indigenous and Spanish heritage and intellect make her an important figure in Mexican history. Her story was introduced to modern audiences by author Octavio Paz.

Sor Juana's writings continue to be studied and celebrated in Mexico, as part of the country's cultural heritage. Moreover, her advocacy for women's rights and her critique of patriarchal structures resonates strongly in contemporary Mexican society, where issues of gender equality and social justice remain relevant.

Sojourner Truth

Sojourner Truth is an essential part of American history. She was born as an enslaved woman and emerged as a formidable force in the abolitionist movement despite being unable to read or write. Much like Hildegard Von Bingen, her life was infused with deep religious beliefs and Christian mysticism. Her primary profession was as an itinerant preacher. She worked as a nurse with the Freedman's Bureau during the Reconstruction era.

Isabella Baumfree was born in Ulster County, New York at the close of the 18th century. She was in the minority 10% African American population in New York State, born when slavery was still legal there. Her parents, Elizabeth and James Baumfree, had roots that traced back to Ghana and Guinea. They had ten of their children sold off, including Isabella who was first sold at age eight for $100.

Isabella's early years were marked by a succession of new owners when she was sold in 1810 to the Dumont family. She endured unspeakable hardships, working as both a domestic servant and nurse for the family. Her first language was Dutch, and her new owners only spoke English. Isabella's personal life was also fraught. She had a daughter, Diana, with a man named Robert, who was enslaved on a neighboring farm. She was not allowed to marry Robert, and was instead married to an older man, Thomas, with whom she had three more children, Peter, Elizabeth, and Sophia.

Although New York outlawed slavery for adults in 1827, her children remained enslaved by the Dumonts. In defiance of this injustice, she took her youngest child, Sophia, and escaped to a neighboring family's home.

Isabella next made another bold move to New York City, where she worked as a maid and as a Pentecostal preacher. When the Dumonts illegally sold Isabella's son Peter to Alabama, she confronted them: "I'll have my child again...I was sure God would help me to get him." With the help of the Quaker church, she secured a decree and successfully brought Peter back to New York under threat of legal punishment for the Dumonts.

In 1832, Isabella joined the Kingdom of Matthias, a church community that came from of the Second Great Awakening, a Pentecostal movement emphasizing mystical experiences. On June 1, 1843, Isabella changed her name to Sojourner Truth and started a new life as an itinerant preacher, saying: "God is to be worshiped at all times and in all places; and one portion of time never seemed to me more holy than another. "

She had a regular practice of praying, speaking, and hearing from God. Although she was Illiterate, she had her children to read the Bible to her. She traveled preaching from town to town throughout New England. She eventually settled in Massachusetts, living in a Christian cooperative community, the Northampton Association for Education and Industry, for thirteen years.

In 1844, Sojourner gave her first anti-slavery speech, a rare woman in the abolitionist movement. She went on a lecture tour, speaking in 22 states in an anti-slavery tour organized by William Lloyd Garrison. Her landmark speech "Ain't I a Woman?", delivered at the 1851 Ohio Women's Rights Convention, is one of the most powerful anti-abolition and feminist speeches in American history. Sojourner spoke about how whites would have to answer to God for the treatment of African Americans. The speech wasn't published until 1863, and it remains controversial how much of the speech was Sojourner's, and how much may have been rewritten by white women to make her language sound more stereotypical. The Sojourner Truth Project highlights the differences between an early written version of her speech,

May I say a few words? I want to say a few words about this matter. I am a woman's rights. I have as much muscle as any man and can do as much work as any man. I have plowed and reaped and husked and chopped and mowed, and can any man do more than that? I have heard much about the sexes being equal; I can carry as much as any man, and can eat as much too, if I can get it. I am as strong as any man that is now. As for intellect, all I can say is, if women have a pint and man a quart - why can't she have her little pint full?

The same section of the famous version was constructed by Dana Frances Gage, and had Sojourner speak in a completely different dialect.

Well, chillen, whar dar's so much racket dar must be som'ting out o'kilter. I tink dat, 'twixt deniggers of de South and de women at de Norf, all a-talking 'bout rights, de white men will be in a fix pretty soon. But what's all this here talking 'bout? Dat man ober dar say dat women needs to be helped into carriages, and lifted over ditches, and to have de best place eberywhar. Nobody eber helps me into carriages or ober mud-puddles, or gives me any best place. And ar'n't I a woman? Look at me. Look at my arm. I have plowed and planted and gathered into barns, and no man could head me. and ar'n't I a woman? I could work as much as eat as much as a man, (when I could get it,) and bear de lash as well, and ar'n't I a woman? I have borne thirteen chillen, and seen 'em mos' all sold off into slavery, and when I cried out with a mother's grief, none but Jesus heard. and ar'n't I a woman?

Sojourner's life story was recorded by others, including her biography by Olive Gilbert and Harriet Beecher Stowe's The Libyan Sibyl. Despite inaccuracies and the biases of her biographers, her impact as an activist, reformer, and public speaker remains undeniable.

When the Civil War broke out in 1861, she worked to support Union efforts through fundraising and met many notable figures like Harriet Tubman, Abraham Lincoln, and Frederick Douglas. After the Civil War, Truth dedicated herself to the National Freedmen's Relief Association, working as a nurse at the Freedmen's Village in Virginia and the Freedmen's Hospital in Washington.

The Freedmen's Bureau was established in 1865 and provided essential services to the formerly enslaved. But it was underfunded and threatened by terrorism until Congress dismantled it in 1872. A letter recounts Sojourner's efforts: "When we follow her from one field of labor to another, her time divided between teaching, preaching, nursing, watching, and praying, ever ready to counsel, comfort, and assist."

She continued to fight against racial segregation and promoted mass migration of African Americans to the West. Sojourner petitioned Congress to pass the 14th amendment, which granted citizenship and equal rights to African Americans, even as the abolitionists and women's rights movement fought over its passage. Many suffragists opposed the amendment if women were not included, while abolitionists wanted it passed as soon as possible.

Sojourner Truth died on November 26, 1883, in Battle Creek, Michigan. Frederick Douglas wrote at her death: "In the death of Sojourner Truth, a marked figure has disappeared from the earth.

Venerable for age, distinguished for insight into human nature, remarkable for independence and courageous self-assertion, devoted to the welfare of her race, she has been for the last forty years an object of respect and admiration to social reformers everywhere."

Mary Seacole

Mary's story begins in Kingston, Jamaica in 1805. We know she was born to a Scottish father and a Jamaican Creole mother although much of her early life remains a mystery. At the time, Jamaica was a British colony starkly divided between a population of 28,000 white inhabitants and the 280,000 of African descent, the majority of whom were enslaved.

Mary's mother was a doctoress and owner of Blundell Hall, a boarding house and hospital. Jamaican doctresses combined West African and Caribbean traditions, prescribed herbal remedies, performed procedures, and provided medical and nursing care, operating in parallel with British colonial medicine. In her autobiography, The Many Adventures of Mary Seacole, Mary recalls practicing doctoring on her dolls as a child. Influenced by both her mother and an anonymous older white patroness who funded her education, Mary was curious and adventurous.

At 16, she traveled to Haiti and Cuba and spent a year in London. "All my life long, I have followed the impulse which led me to be up and doing; and so far from resting idle anywhere, I have never wanted inclination to rove, nor will powerful enough to carry out my wishes."

Mary's book primarily chronicles her adventures abroad leaving out many important Jamaican events, like the 1831 Christmas rebellion, where 20,000 slaves led a mutiny, and the 1834 abolishment of slavery. It also omits much of her personal life, except her unusual interracial marriage to Edwin Horatio Hamilton Seacole.

The 1840s were a decade of tragedy for Mary when her patroness, mother ,and husband all died. A cholera epidemic, which causes severe diarrhea that kills 50% of the infected, killed nearly 10% of the Jamaican population. Mary cared for people throughout the epidemic. In 1843 a fire destroyed Blundell Hall and much of Kingston.

After these losses, Mary left Jamaica, working as an entrepreneur and doctoress across Haiti, the Caribbean, and Central America. She visited her brother in Panama, who ran a store selling supplies to those headed for the California Gold Rush. In a remote Panamanian outpost along the Chagres River, Mary's nursing skills were indispensable during another cholera outbreak. She was the sole person experienced in treating the disease, applying the scientific method to improve her treatments and surviving an infection herself. She opened The British Hotel, a boarding house/hospital like Blundell Hall, traveling between Panama and Jamaica to oversee them both.

In 1853, Jamaica faced a yellow fever outbreak, and Mary was commissioned to run a British military hospital. Having cared for soldiers for years, she considered herself a loyal subject of the British Empire. She wrote of her experience during this epidemic:"I do not willingly care to dwell upon scenes of suffering and death, but it is with such scenes that my life's experience has made me most familiar. Death is always terrible—no one need be ashamed to fear it."

Her next journey took her to the Crimean War, a trip she financed her herself. "I made up my mind that if the army wanted nurses, they would be glad of me, and with all the ardor of my nature, which ever carried me where inclination prompted, I decided that I would go to the Crimea, and go I did."

Florence Nightingale was also headed to the Crimea, appointed by the British War Office to head a field hospital in Scutari. Nightingale was 34 and had been nursing for 17 years, having trained at the Kaiserswerth hospital and served as a Nursing Superintendent in Britain. As the head of the field hospital, Nightingale handpicked her staff and maintained strict control, including the exclusion of non-white nurses. Soon after arriving, Mary walked up to the hospital to volunteer with Florence Nightingale, who refused her offer.

Instead, Mary decided to open a third British Hotel for soldiers and the wounded with funds she raised herself. She partnered with a man that she had worked with in Panama. She spent six weeks living aboard a docked ship in Scutari, fundraising, selling goods, and caring for soldiers. Mary's autobiography was written to appeal to the British public, and didn't include her full story. One historian also discusses the likelihood that the companion she discusses in her book may have been a hidden daughter, Sally.

Mary's autobiography records her experiences:"I wonder if I can ever forget the scenes I witnessed there? I declare that I saw rough bearded men stand by and cry like the softest-hearted women at the sight of suffering they saw. I have often heard men talk and preach very learnedly and conclusively about the great wickedness and selfishness of the human heart; I used to wonder whether they would have modified those opinions if they had been my companions for one day of the six weeks I spent upon the wharf and seen but one day's experience of the Christian sympathy and brotherly love shown by the strong to the weak."

Mary stayed in the Crimea for a year following a grueling daily routine: up at dawn to prepare food and medications, with breakfast at 7, patients arriving at 9, visiting officers in the hospital, and providing meals throughout the day, closing the hotel at 8 pm for a rare moment of relaxation. She fought rumors of gambling and drunkenness at her establishment, emphasizing her commitment to moral conduct.

The Crimean War ended in March 1856 with the defeat of the Russians. Mary moved to London, writing and publishing The Wonderful Adventures of Mrs. Seacole in Many Lands before returning to Jamaica in 1860. She became one of the most well-known figures in England, befriending the Prince of Wales and inspiring a military festival in her honor that drew 80,000 attendees.

Mary Seacole died in London at age 76. She had transformed herself into a heroine of the Crimean War, a supporter of the British Empire, an entrepreneur, and a dedicated and ambitious nurse. Her popularity surged in the UK at the end of the 20th Century with a documentary and a reappraisal of black history, along with the republication of her book in 1984.

Margaret Fuller

Margaret Fuller was a pioneering intellectual and one of the most influential thinkers of 19th-century America. A champion for women's rights, education, and personal freedom, she was a writer, educator, and activist, and a vocal advocate for gender equality. As the first American female foreign correspondent, she documented the events of the Italian Revolution while working as a nurse and running a hospital for soldiers.

Sarah Margaret Fuller was born in Massachusetts in 1810, the eldest of eight children of Timothy Fuller, a Harvard lawyer and Congressman who guided her first-rate education. Educated at home and the Boston Lyceum, she studied French, German, Italian, Latin, and Greek, classical history and literature. Margaret's confidence and boldness clashed with the societal norms set for women at the time. As a teenager, unable to attend university, she developed an interest in German romanticism, translating works of Kant and Goethe. She defied expectations by not marrying, choosing instead to earn her living as a journalist and writer, first publishing in 1834.

Her passion for German philosophy and literature led her to become a central figure in the transcendentalist movement. The first major American intellectual movement, the philosophy adapted German romanticism and celebrated nature, individualism and idealism. The Transcendentalist Club, which first met in 1836, included Ralph Waldo Emerson, William Lloyd Garrison, and Henry David Thoreau.

Margaret developed a deep friendship with Emerson in 1835, the same year her father died of cholera and left her family destitute. Margaret had to support her mother and younger siblings by teaching at Bronson Alcott's Temple School and translating work. Margaret also started Conversations, organizing paid educational opportunities to women on topics like Greek mythology.

In 1840, she became the editor of Emerson's influential journal, *The Dial.* During this time, she wrote some of the earliest works of American feminism, including her book, Women in the Nineteenth Century. In 1846, Margaret left *The Dial* to write for the abolitionist newspaper the *New York Tribune* and traveled to Europe as America's first female foreign correspondent.

After traveling through England and France she settled in Rome, where Italy was divided and under the rule of the Hapsburg Empire. Shortly after arriving in Rome, she met the Marquise Giovanni Angelo Ossoli on Easter 1847 in St. Peter's Square. Native Roman Ossoli was eight years younger, deeply Catholic, and not well-educated. But Margaret was in love, writing,:"Once I was almost all intellect. Now I am almost all feeling."

Their love story unfolded against t"e backdrop of the 1848 Italian Revolution, which aimed to free and unite the country. In addition to reporting, Margaret became a supporter of the revolution. She was hiding her pregnancy while Ossoli, a soldier in the Roman Civil Guard, waited to be called to fight.

On September 5th, Margaret gave birth to their son, Angelo Eugenio Filippo Ossoli, with Giovanni by her side. She left the baby with a foster family to keep him safe in the country and returned to Rome, visiting him when she could.

When the Austrian and French armies marched into Rome the following spring, Margaret was appointed Regolatrice of the Hospital of Fate Bene Fratelli. The Provisional Government of the Roman Republic had formed a committee that entrusted her with organizing care for the sick and the wounded revolutionary soldiers. She wrote in the *Tribune*:"War near at hand seems to me even more dreadful than I had fancied it. I have for the first time seen what wounded men suffer. The night of the 30th of April I passed in the hospital and saw the terrible agonies of those dying or who needed amputation, felt their mental pains and longing for their loved ones."

She wrote a letter to Emerson: "Since April 30th, I go almost daily to the hospitals, and thought I have suffered, for I had no idea, before, how terrible gunshot wounds and wound fever are – yet I have taken pleasure, great pleasure in being with the men. There is scarcely one who is not moved by a noble spirit."

Other observers wrote their recollections of her during this time: "Her health was feeble and delicate, the dead and dying around her in every form of pain and horror, but she never shrank from the duty she had assumed. Her heart and soul were in the cause for which these men had fought, and all was done that women could do to comfort them in their suffering."

This initial revolution failed and the French took over Rome, putting Margaret and Ossoli in grave danger. Margaret escaped to reclaim Angelo, only to find him neglected and half-starved by his foster family. Giovanni also managed to escape the city, and the parents nursed him back to health.

After this harrowing year, Margaret decided to write to her mother about Angelo and their son, claiming she was married, although it remains unclear if this was legal. Their small family fled to Florence, as Giovanni had lost everything in his support of the revolution and Margaret was fired from the Tribune due to her pregnancy.

Planning to return to the U.S. with her family and publish her book on the Roman Revolution, Margaret celebrated her 40th birthday on their tragic journey home. There was a smallpox outbreak that killed the captain and Nino became very ill. A terrible storm caused the ship to wreck just off Fire Island, New York. Margaret, Giovanni, and Nino all drowned, and her book on the Roman revolution was lost.

Margaret Fuller's untimely death leaves room to speculate on the impact her exceptional intellect might have had. Her work sparked critical conversations on equality that resonated far beyond her lifetime. Though her life was brief, Fuller's influence as a thinker and reformer continues to shape discussions about justice and gender equality today.

Bridget "Biddy" Mason

By the time Bridget "Biddy" Mason died in 1891, she was a respected philanthropist and one of the first residents in the city of Los Angeles. Biddy was born in 1818 enslaved in Georgia. She was sold to the owners of a Mississippi plantation before she was old enough to know her mother and was again sold to Robert and Rebecca Smith. She was not able to read or write but learned nursing, midwifery, and herbal medicine through hands-on learning and used it to treat both black and white patients.

As a midwife, she attended the births of all six of Robert and Rebecca Smith's children. In 1848 Robert Smith converted to Mormonism, taking his family and those he owned to follow Brigham Young. When they left the South, Biddy had three children: Ellen, 10, Ann, 4 and baby Harriet, who were likely fathered by Robert Smith.

A ninety-person wagon train, one third of them enslaved, traveled to Utah on a two-thousand-mile, seven-month journey. They spent two years living in Salt Lake City, where slavery was still legal, before moving on to the newly established state of California.

In 1851, the families traveled to San Bernardino to purchase land and establish a Mormon colony. The settler population was growing rapidly, attracted by land grants that displaced Mexican and

Indigenous populations. At the time, Los Angeles was a small town of 1600 people and fewer than twenty African Americans.

Although slavery had been illegal in California since 1850, the law was not enforced and the Smiths were able to keep Biddy, her friend Hannah and their children enslaved. Like the rest of the country, the Fugitive Slave Act was enforced in California, meaning that Hannah and Biddy faced the risk of arrest if they attempted to escape. Soon after their arrival, California enacted laws that emancipated slaves brought into the state, but neither Hannah nor Biddy would have been aware of these changes.

In 1856, Smith decided to move his family to Texas, so he could continue his ownership. The women met Charles Rowan, a formerly enslaved teamster and anti-slavery advocate living in the city, who encouraged the women to legally contest their enslavement. The move to Texas was delayed because Hannah was pregnant with her eighth child, allowing the women time to legally fight for their rights.

When the group did attempt to leave Los Angeles, sheriffs pursued the Smiths, and Hannah, Biddy, and their children were placed in the county jail to ensure they could not be taken out of state before their case was heard in court. The details of how this came about remains unclear, but it is likely that free Black residents of Los Angeles played a pivotal role in the legal proceedings that would secure their freedom.

According to reports from the *Los Angeles Star*, their trial took place in January 1856. Their freedom was unlikely as Smith and his lawyers lied, threatened, bribed and even attempted kidnapping to keep them enslaved. Biddy was left unrepresented in court during the trial as her lawyer had been bribed to not appear. As an African American, she was not able to speak in court on her own behalf. The presiding judge, Judge Hayes, a former slave owner, subverted the racist law and interviewed Biddy in his chambers, allowing her to speak for herself. He ruled against Smith and freed everyone, stopping their forced move to Texas.

Such a rare case of legal justice for African Americans in the U.S. would have been impossible if it had taken place just a year later. The 1857 Supreme Court Dred Scott decision ruled that citizenship, and constitutional rights did not extend to free African Americans. After being freed, Biddy faced the challenge of supporting herself and her family. She owned nothing and could not read or write. She was always at risk of re-enslavement, and so she always kept her papers with her. Biddy's daughter Ellen Mason married Charles Owen, and they all moved in with the Owen's family.

For ten years Biddy worked as a nurse and assistant to Dr. John Griffins, Judge Hayes's brother-in-law. She took care of patients at the jail for $2.50 a week, worked as a midwife delivering hundreds of babies, and provided nursing care during a smallpox outbreak. She used these earnings to buy a piece of land, making her the first African American female landowner in L.A. She continued to buy land throughout her life.

A devout Christian, she helped found the First African Methodist Episcopal Church, which still has 18,000 members to this day. She owned the land that housed the first African American public school in Los Angeles. Biddy died on January 15, 1891, at the age of 72, and was worth $300,000 (millions in today's dollars). She used her nursing to build a legacy as a healer, philanthropist, and community leader, helping shape the city of Los Angeles.

Walt Whitman

Walt Whitman, one of America's greatest poets, was born in 1819 to a Quaker farming family on Long Island and raised in Brooklyn. He left school at the age of eleven, taking on various jobs such as office boy, schoolteacher, and printer's apprentice. In his twenties and thirties, Whitman edited and wrote for several newspapers in New York City and New Orleans. Whitman was inspired to become a poet after hearing Ralph Waldo Emerson speak on the importance of poetry. His inspiration was America and the vibrancy of New York City, writing: "Remember, my life in Brooklyn and New York, absorbing a million people with an intimacy, an eagerness, an abandon."

Although Whitman spent his entire life based in New York, a journey down the Mississippi River to New Orleans inspired him to write his great work, Leaves of Grass. He worked on the first edition between 1847 and 1855, publishing it just before his 36th birthday. Whitman's writing celebrated sexual freedom, openly discussing masturbation, queerness, and sexual fluidity, far outside the norms of conservative American culture. He boldly wrote:

Without shame the man I like now

and avows the deliciousness of his sex

without shame the woman I like knows and avows hers

I am a poet of the body

And I am a poet of the soul

Have you supposed it is beautiful to be born?

I tell you I know it is just as beautiful to die;

for I take my death with the dying and my birth with the newborn babe

I am the poet of sin

For I do not believe in sin

His journey into nursing started as a reporter visiting New York hospitals at the beginning of the Civil War. In 1862, he traveled to Fredericksburg to spend two weeks with his brother George while he recovered in a Union Army Camp, but ended up staying for several years. He worked in the Department of the Interior in the mornings and spent afternoons comforting the wounded in military hospitals. Professionally trained and untrained nurses worked side by side in the hospitals, giving medication, feeding patients, and spending time with wounded soldiers.

Whitman wrote about his experience in the hospitals for *New York Times* and *Brooklyn Daily Eagle*, war poetry and several books, Democratic Vistas (1870) and Memoranda During the War (1875). Whitman considered himself a "consolant" of the wounded, curing people with affection. He wrote letters for afflicted soldiers, dressed wounds, distributed gifts of money, clothing, and food, and read aloud to them. He found this work and experience to be life changing, inspired by the wounded soldiers and the profound emotions of the war, "the very centre, circumference, umbilicus, of my whole career."

Whitman stood out. Another nurse, Amanda Aiken, described him in detail in her diary: "Walt Whitman visits our hospital almost daily. He took a fancy to my fever boy and would watch with him sometimes half the night. He is a poet, and I believe has written some very queer books about 'Free Love,' etc.....He is an odd-looking genius, with a heavy frame, tall, with a turned-down Byronic collar, high head with straggling hair, and very pink rims to his eyes. When he stalks down the ward, I feel the 'prickings of my thumbs,' and never speak to him." The following passage from his poem the Wound Dresser is a wonderful description from this time:

Bearing the bandages, water and sponge,

Straight and swift to my wounded I go,

Where they lie on the ground after the battle brought in,

Where their priceless blood reddens the grass, the ground,

Or to the rows of the hospital tent, or under the roof'd hospital,

To the long rows of cots up and down each side I return,

To each and all one after another I draw near, not one do I miss,

An attendant follows holding a tray, he carries a refuse pail,

Soon to be fill'd with clotted rags and blood, emptied, and fill'd again.

I onward go, I stop, With hinged knees and steady hand to dress wounds,

I am firm with each, the pangs are sharp yet unavoidable,

One turns to me his appealing eyes—poor boy!

I never knew you,

Yet I think I could not refuse this moment to die for you, if that
would save you.

The energy Whitman poured into nursing took a toll on his health and he became more conventional and conservative after the war. Although very well known, he felt he didn't achieve the success he deserved and found it difficult to find meaning and purpose. Increased sexual repression and obscenity laws also restricted his work. Additional editions of Leaves of Grass were published in 1867 and 1871. In 1873, after suffering a stroke, he moved to Camden, New Jersey, to live with his family. Despite his health challenges, Whitman continued to travel and write, meeting Oscar Wilde in 1882 during Wilde's trip to the U.S. Whitman's biographer and friend, Horace Traubel, a radical socialist visited him daily for ten years.

By 1888, Whitman had recurrent strokes and needed full-time care. During these years, he destroyed almost all his personal correspondence, adding to the mystery about who he really was and with who he may have been romantically involved. He died in 1892 at the age of 73, completing his final edition of Leaves of Grass just before his death.

Whitman's poetry tried to contain the full spectrum of humanity complexity. His experience caring for soldiers deeply influenced this work. Whitman articulated a vision of a world that is free, sensual, and alive. Whitman's time as a nurse during war allowed him to see humanity at its most vulnerable, and the experience deepened his understanding of humanity and shaped his writing.

Harriet Tubman

Even though she is a well-known name in American history, Harriet Tubman's impact and accomplishments are perhaps the most extraordinary in this book. Born Araminta Ross around 1820 in the Chesapeake Bay area of Maryland, Tubman entered the world enslaved, the granddaughter of an African woman named Mercy. Her parents, Henry and Rit Ross, were able to stay together but were separated from their children.

At age five, Araminta was leased to neighbors for childcare and housework. Frequently beaten and malnourished, she was returned to her parents when too weak to work, nursed back to health, and sent out again. As an adolescent, she was nearly killed when an overseer hit her, causing a severe head injury that left her with permanent damage. Biographers speculate that the mystical visions she experienced were seizures resulting from these injuries.

Harriet's father was freed at age 45. Her mother and some siblings should have been freed at the same time, but their owners refused to honor their legal rights. In 1844, Harriet married freeman John Tubman. After her owner sold two of her sisters down south, she decided to run away. She told her biographer, Sarah Bradford, about her decision: "I had reasoned this out in my mind, there was one of two things I had a right to, liberty, or death. If I could not have one, I would have the other, for no man should take me alive. I should fight for my liberty as long as my strength lasted, and when the time came for me to go, the Lord would let them take me."

In the fall of 1849, Araminta ran away with her brothers Ben and Henry, but returned when they decided they couldn't leave their families. A month later, she left again, alone, and was supported by the Underground Railroad as she walked ninety miles to Philadelphia, adopting the name Harriet Tubman. The Underground Railroad, which began in the 1830s, was an informal network of abolitionist Quakers protecting runaway slaves from fugitive slave laws. These laws became increasingly stringent over sixty years, culminating in the passage of the Fugitive Slave Act of 1850. This federal law overruled other anti-slavery regulations, criminalizing assistance to escaped slaves and empowering slave catchers to operate freely across the entire United States. The act imposed heavy penalties on those who aided runaway slaves and mandated that all citizens, regardless of personal beliefs, assist in their capture. This escalation not only exacerbated tensions between the north and south but also intensified the dangers faced by escaped slaves and their allies, leading to greater involvement in the Underground Railroad and resistance movements.

After escaping, Harriet returned to Maryland to save her family. She received word that her niece, Kizzy, was to be sold with her children. Her husband asked for help after he managed to buy Kizzy and their two children. Harriet smuggled them to safety, preventing their recapture. She traveled to Maryland again in 1851 to rescue her husband, but he had taken another wife and refused to see her.

Over many trips, she rescued most of her family, including her parents, and helped them reach Canada, which had passed policies to protect fugitive slaves and generally refused to extradite them to the U.S. Harriet was unique within the Underground

Railroad as she not only supported refugees but also personally traveled to the South to help rescue them, transporting groups of up to 15 people at a time.

Tubman made a trip south each fall, spending the rest of the year with her family in Canada. Thomas Garrett, an abolitionist and leader of the Underground Railroad, stated, "Harriett has confidence that God will protect her from harm in all her perilous journeys. I never met with any person of any color who had more confidence in the voice of God, as spoken direct to her soul."

Harriet was also involved with the abolitionist movement and supported the radical John Brown, who was planning a slave uprising to end slavery. He viewed slavery as a sin that justified violence to end the practice. Brown was responsible for a massacre of slave owners in Pottawatomie, Kansas. Brown and Tubman's relationship was based on their Christian faith and anti-slavery views, with Tubman supporting him through fundraising and her knowledge of the area. Brown was executed after his planned raid on Harpers Ferry in 1859, an event that helped trigger the Civil War.

In the final years before the Civil War, Harriet purchased a farm in upstate New York, saying, "God's time is always near. He set the North Star in the heavens; He gave me the strength in my limbs. He meant I should be free." Despite being a wanted fugitive, she traveled around the North, speaking, advocating, and fundraising for abolition. Her last rescue mission was to free her sister Rachel, who died before Harriet reached her, so Tubman rescued seven other people instead.

While the abolition of slavery now seems inevitable, it was a radical idea prior to the Civil War and was not supported by President Lincoln or the country. Tubman made it clear that slavery must be abolished completely, without compromise. She described her views: "Suppose there was an awfully big snake down there on the floor. He bites you. You send for the doctor to cure the bite, but the snake, he coils up there, and while the doctor is doing it, he bites you again. The doctor cuts down that bite, but while he is doing it the snake springs up and bites you again, and so he keeps doing it till you kill him. That's what Mister Lincoln ought to know."

In 1860, Lincoln was elected to the presidency and South Carolina seceded from the union and started the Civil War. Harriet immediately joined the war effort. In the spring of 1862, the Union Army invaded Port Royal, South Carolina. Fleeing slave owners left behind ten thousand people. Harriet traveled to South Carolina to work with these refugees, serving as a nurse, caring for patients in the hospital, and working in public health.

While working as a nurse at a Union army hospital in Port Royal, Harriet helped create a spy network that conducted the 1863 Combahee River Raid. During this raid, 150 black Union soldiers freed 750 slaves from coastal plantations. She was the first woman to lead an armed military expedition during the Civil War. She continued working as a nurse caring for black soldiers even while serving as a spy. Harriet was very critical of Lincoln and the Union Army for the unequal treatment in hospitals, where Blacks died at 2.5 times the rate of white soldiers.

In February 1865, the Thirteenth Amendment to the Constitution formally abolished slavery in the United States. Despite her extraordinary heroism and contributions during the Civil War, Harriet did not receive her rightful war pension. She had to fight for many years to receive her $12 per month and wasn't paid until 1899.

After the Civil War, she became actively involved in the women's rights movement, giving speeches and attending suffrage events to share her experiences, the capabilities of women, and how they deserved the same rights as men. Harriet worked alongside prominent suffragists such as Susan B. Anthony and Elizabeth Cady Stanton, and she was a member of the National Federation of Afro-American Women.

Harriet's remarkable life and legacy were chronicled by Sarah H. Bradford in her biography, Harriet, the Moses of Her People, published in 1886. While this book helped to raise awareness about Tubman's contributions the book is also riddled with inaccuracies. In her later years, Harriet settled on her farm in Auburn, New York, where she dedicated herself to humanitarian efforts. She established the Harriet Tubman Home for the Aged, which provided care for elderly African Americans who had nowhere else to go.

Harriet passed away on March 10, 1913, but her impact on American history endures. Her moral leadership and unmatched bravery exemplify the power of resilience, courage, and unwavering dedication to justice. Her legacy of moral leadership and bravery are an inspiration for advocates for equality and justice everywhere.

Kusumoto Ine

For nearly two hundred years, Japan deliberately isolated itself from the rest of the world. From 1640 to 1850 employees of the Dutch United East Indian Company were the only people allowed to interact with the Japanese. The Dutch could only exchange goods and information off the coast of Nagasaki and during a once-a-year visit to Edo (Tokyo). In 1823, Phillip Franz Von Siebold, a German physician, botanist, and traveler came to work in Nagasaki as a part of this agreement. He opened a clinic and taught medicine, botany, chemistry, and physics. During his time in Japan, he fathered a daughter, Ine, with a teenage Japanese courtesan, Kusumoto Taki, in 1827.

Soon after, Siebold was accused of spying and banished from Japan, although he continued to support Kusumoto and their daughter, sending letters and books. Ine frequently traveled to Dejima Island to watch for ships and her father's return. Ine was educated as a traditional Japanese woman, learning the tea ceremony, dancing, and flower arranging but could not help but stand out in the very homogeneous Japan.

At 18, Ine left home to study midwifery and general practice in the rangaku, or Western medical tradition. Nineteenth century Japan had multiple healthcare traditions, including mystical Shinto, Chinese medicine, Kampo, and Rangaku. She studied under Ishii Soken, an apprentice of her father, in Okayama. She likely began her apprenticeship as a servant, learning through hands-on experience over several years. The apprenticeship ended when Soken raped and impregnated Ine.

Ine remained determined to study, raising her daughter, Tada, with her mother's help, and refused any support from Soken. She accepted support from her father's network and studied obstetrics for another three years, before opening her own general practice and midwifery clinic in Nagasaki.

In 1853, the U.S. Navy fleet led by Commodore Matthew Perry pressured Japan to open to foreign trade, leading to the period known as the Meji Restoration. Ine gained new career opportunities when her father was pardoned and returned to Japan in 1859. She worked with her father and other European doctors, including Pompe van Meerdervoort, who praised her abilities and noted that Siebold's students held her in very high esteem. She participated in dissections, assisted in operations, and worked in the women's ward at the Nagasaki Yôjôsho, a Western-style hospital. Three years after Siebold returned he was again banished from Japan, dying in Europe.

Ine was respected within both scholarly samurai circles and centers of Western learning. She was honored with a rice stipend for her service to Date Munenari, the daimyo of Uwajima and had students under her tutelage. In 1867, Ine played a crucial role in attending the childbirth of the daimyo's wife, Yoshiko with two male doctors, although both mother and child died after the delivery.

In 1870, Ine moved to Edo just as Western medicine and public health were being widely adopted throughout the country. The government began to professionalize and standardize health care and the first medical school opened. Licensure to practice medical care, nursing, and midwifery became formalized, requiring examinations and standardized training, rather than apprenticeship. In a recurring pattern seen in many places, the newly professionalized fields were restricted to men. Ine, as an informally trained woman, obtained a license as a midwife so she could continue limited practice.

She raised her daughter as a single mother, never married, and passed away in 1903. While Ine did not write her own story and we only know some of the details of her life, her remarkable story is the topic Yoshimura Akira's 1978 novel *Von Siebold's Daughter*. Ine used the upheaval in nineteenth-century Japan to create an extraordinary life and career that defied the limitations of her time.

Louisa May Alcott

Louisa May Alcott, author of the beloved novel Little Women, was a writer, abolitionist, educator and served as a nurse in the Civil War. Born in 1832 in Germantown, Pennsylvania, she was the second of four daughters in the unconventional and often struggling household of Bronson and Abby Alcott. While Little Women introduces readers to Jo March, the independent heroine inspired by Alcott herself, the book did not include many of the real-life challenges she faced.

Her father made his living as an itinerant teacher, philosopher, and education reformer. The family was abolitionist and her father's Temple School was closed when he attempted to enroll an African American. Like Margaret Fuller, Bronson Alcott was a key figure in the Transcendentalist movement, a progressive mid-19th-century philosophy rooted in New England. This intellectual circle included luminaries such as Ralph Waldo Emerson, Nathaniel Hawthorne, Henry David Thoreau, Walt Whitman, and Herman Melville, whose ideas and writings shaped American thought and culture.

Bronson Alcott's unyielding idealism drove him to pursue ventures like Fruitlands, a utopian farm where the family lived when Louisa was ten. Co-founded with Charles Lane, Fruitlands was envisioned as a self-sustaining vegan community. However, Lane's insistence on celibacy and his interference in Bronson and Abby's marriage quickly unraveled the experiment. The utopia collapsed. Bronson suffered a nervous breakdown, but ultimately chose his family over his radical aspirations.

In 1857, the Alcotts returned to Concord, Massachusetts, moving into Orchard House, which later became the setting for *Little Women*, and can still be visited today. Soon after, her family significantly changed: her sister Lizzie died of complications from rheumatic fever; her older sister Anna married; and her youngest sister May moved to Boston. Louisa lived for a short period in Boston, but returned to Concord to help care for her ill mother.

Amid their family struggles, the Alcott family was deeply engaged in the abolitionist movement. They sheltered a fugitive slave in their home, risking legal consequences to fight against slavery. After the execution of John Brown—a fervent abolitionist who led the ill-fated raid on Harpers Ferry to spark a slave uprising—the Alcotts offered Brown's widow and children refuge.

In 1861, the same year she finished her first novel, Moods, Louisa volunteered as a nurse in the Union army. Under the strict supervision of Dorothea Dix, the superintendent of female nurses, Louisa began working at Union Hotel Hospital in Washington, D.C. Her experience was both physically and emotionally grueling, exposing her to the stark realities of war and the systematic mistreatment of African Americans.

In her memoir of that time, Hospital Sketches, Alcott provides vivid accounts of what she witnessed. Reflecting on her first encounters with the casualties of war, she wrote: "The suffering is indescribable. The sight of several stretchers, each with its legless, armless, or desperately wounded occupant, entering the ward, admonished me that I was there to work, not to wonder or weep."

Despite her resolve, Alcott's nursing career was short-lived. After just six weeks of service, she contracted typhoid fever, a common illness in the unsanitary hospital environment. The mercury-based treatment she received left her permanently weakened and would cause her problems for the rest of her life.

Her father traveled to D.C. when she was near death and brought her back to Massachusetts to gradually recover. Although she never returned to war nursing, the experience left a mark, deepening her empathy and her social conscience. She did use her nursing skills further when she accepted a position accompanying a wealthy invalid to Europe.

Financial pressures compelled her to write to support her family. She reluctantly agreed to write a novel for young girls at the suggestion of her publisher, Thomas Niles, because she needed the money. Alcott completed the first part of Little Women in just two months, drawing inspiration from her own family and childhood to write the story of the four March sisters—Meg, Jo, Beth, and Amy. Published when Louisa was 36 years old in 1868, the book became an instant success, earning her $1,000—a significant sum at the time.

Though Little Women brought her financial success and celebrity, her family was marked by loss, and she struggled with her health. Her mother died in 1877. Louisa took on the care of her niece, Louisa "Lulu" May Nieriker, after the death of her younger sister, May Alcott Nieriker, in 1879. May had passed away shortly after giving birth in Paris, leaving a letter requesting that Louisa raise her daughter. Despite her own health challenges and busy literary career, Louisa devoted herself to Lulu, never having children of her own. Louisa never married and her sexuality remains a mystery. Scholars have speculated that she may have identified as a lesbian or even as a transgendered man, as she wrote of her disconnection from traditional female roles, writing in her journal: "I long to be a man... I was born with a boy's nature, a boy's spirit, and a boy's wrath."

Louisa continued writing and activism for the rest of her life. She helped found the Women's Educational and Industrial Union in Boston to support impoverished women. Louisa died at age 55 in 1888, just two days after her father.

Louisa was a prolific writer, her body of work included over 30 books and collections, as well as nearly 200 short stories and articles. Best known for Little Women and its sequels, she wrote a variety of novels, including An Old-Fashioned Girl and Eight Cousins, that explored themes of family, morality, and independence. Alcott also published gothic stories under the pseudonym A.M. Barnard. Her writing not only entertained but also challenged societal norms of women's roles, independence, and ambition.

Lavinia Dock

Lavinia Lloyd Dock dedicated her nursing career to driving reform from within organizations. She used political influence to create a lasting impact on the nursing profession and its educational standards. Lavinia was a contemporary of Lillian Wald and Emma Goldman, and they shared many of the same ideals, women's participation in politics through suffrage; labor rights; and achieving social equity through nursing work.

Born in 1858 into a wealthy white Pennsylvania family, Lavinia's life was set to follow the predictable patterns of her class and gender. The death of her mother when she was just eighteen prompted a radical redirection. Rejecting the conventional path of marriage and motherhood, Lavinia instead chose to study at the Bellevue Hospital School of Nursing in New York City—a decision that would set the course for a lifetime of professional and political engagement.

Lavinia began her nursing career caring for immigrant patients in New York and serving as a supervisor at a yellow fever hospital, gaining first-hand experience in public health.

Her work expanded when she joined Lillian Wald's Henry Street Settlement, a pioneering organization dedicated to providing healthcare and education to underserved communities. At Henry Street, Lavinia found her true purpose in preventive care and health education, focusing on empowering immigrant families with knowledge and resources to improve their well-being. This experience deepened her commitment to addressing social determinants of health and inspired her activism for broader healthcare reform.

Lavinia was one of the first nurse academics in America. She was named assistant superintendent of nurses at the newly established Johns Hopkins Hospital in 1890, one of the first nursing schools in the country. She taught first-year classes and provided clinical instruction. She wrote some of the earliest nursing textbooks. Her *Materia Medica for Nurses* was the first nurses' manual on drugs. She also wrote *History of Nursing* (co-authored with Mary Adelaide Nutting). In 1910, she published *Hygiene and Mortality*, advocating for the rights and healthcare of sex workers.

For two decades in New York, Lavinia actively engaged in the fight for rights, championing multiple political causes. She worked within the National Women's Party, the radical wing of the suffrage movement, and was an active member of the Women's Trade Union League. She joined with 20,000 female garment workers in the largest women's labor strike in the U.S., the New York shirtwaist strike. In 1912, She joined fellow suffragettes and marched 150 miles from New York City to Albany, demanding the right to vote.

Her activism wasn't merely symbolic. She was jailed multiple times for her demonstrations, including once for attempting to vote in 1896. "It was a great joy to do a little guerilla war in that cause," she wrote, "and I believe that going to jail gave me a purer feeling of unalloyed content than I ever had in any of my other work."

She was disappointed by nurses' disinterest in mobilizing for widespread political engagement. In 1908, the American Nurses Association initially opposed women's right to vote, believing that nurses should remain apolitical. Lavinia wrote a scathing letter against this vote, helping to change the organization's mind:"I cannot help but express my shock and humiliation that nurses could not be depended upon to take instinctively the intelligent and above all the sympathetic position on large human questions." She recognized the crucial importance of political engagement and full citizenship for the nursing profession, understanding that nursing was inherently political.

In 1920, the 19th Amendment was ratified, granting white women the right to vote—though her dream of a politically active nursing corps has never been realized. Lavinia's influence was also global in reach. In 1899, she and fellow nurse Ethel Gordon Fenwick founded the International Council of Nurses, an organization that continues to shape the global nursing profession today.

Lavinia's vision for nursing encompassed the pursuit of independence and professionalization within the field, along with fostering solidarity with the marginalized members of society. She supported Martha Franklin and Adah Thoms in the founding of the National Association of Colored Graduate Nurses, a critical response to the exclusion of African American nurses from state and national nursing organizations.

In 1922, at the age of fifty, Lavinia withdrew from public life, retreating to her family farm in Pennsylvania with her four unmarried sisters. When she passed away in 1956, she left behind a legacy of institutions, activism, and a profession strengthened by her efforts. In Lavinia Dock, we see a life that was not content with merely existing within the systems of her time but one that strove to redefine them.

Lillian Wald

Lillian Wald was the founder of public health nursing and a visionary who redefined what it meant to care for a community. A teacher, radical activist, and trailblazer, Lillian established the Henry Street Settlement, a hub of social reform that continues to thrive in New York City today. With a bold belief in merging professional nursing with social justice, she championed a model of care that addressed not just illness, but the societal conditions that fueled it.

Lillian was born in 1867 in Ohio to a family of German Jewish immigrants. Her family later relocated to Rochester, New York, where they became successful merchants. This prosperity allowed her to enjoy a culturally rich and well-educated childhood.

Lillian was first drawn to nursing after attending her sister's childbirth. "I feel the need of serious, definite work." She refused to get married and traveled widely before entering nursing school, lying about her age to enroll in New York Hospital Training School for Nurses in 1889. She graduated two years later and started work in a juvenile asylum and taught a class in nursing to immigrants.

Initially, Lillian Wald was too overwhelmed with her nursing duties to engage in political activism. "While there, the long hours on duty and the exhausting demands of the ward scarcely allowed freedom for keeping informed as to what was happening in the world outside. It is not strange, therefore, that I should have been ignorant of the various movements which reflected the awakening of the social conscience of the time."

A pivotal moment in her life came when she began working as a nurse in the tenements of the Lower East Side, where she witnessed firsthand the harsh realities of poverty and inequality. "To my inexperience it seemed certain that these conditions were allowed because people didn't know." The tenements were overcrowded, poorly lit, and lacked proper ventilation. Families lived in cramped, dark rooms with inadequate plumbing and sanitation facilities. These conditions led to the rapid spread of diseases such as cholera, tuberculosis, and malaria.

Lillian and her friend Mary Brewster moved into the Eastern European Jewish community to work as nurses. Lillian believed that "nursing collapsed the class consciousness." Lillian initially became involved with the Christian Social Gospel movement, which sought to apply Christian principles to address social issues and advocate for justice.

Inspired by the pioneering work of Jane Addams at Hull House in Chicago, Lillian started a non-religious based visiting nurse service. She worked to professionalize nursing and promote public health nursing and racial inclusiveness. With the support of wealthy banker Jacob Schiff, their nursing service rapidly expanded, eventually reaching all five boroughs and providing care to 1,100 patients annually.

Lillian's political skills helped her to both collaborate with and criticize city officials, health departments, and other powerful political figures. She influenced health policy and championed the role of the school nurse, helping found the Bureau of Child Hygiene. She lobbied the Board of Education to offer school lunch programs and provide education for children with disabilities. In 1903, Lillian helped to create the National Women's Trade Union League that fought for the rights of immigrant garment workers, the eradication of child labor, and the establishment of a minimum wage.

Lillian was also involved in the civil rights movement, urging Jacob Schiff to contribute to the formation of the National Association for the Advancement of Colored People (NAACP). The Henry Street office became an early meeting site for WEB Dubois and the NAACP, the oldest and largest civil rights organization in the United States. Jewish, female, African American, and progressive activists collaborated to champion equality for all individuals and work toward the elimination of racial prejudice.

In 1910, Lillian embarked on a six-month world tour, traveling to Hawaii, Japan, China, and Russia, to promote peace and internationalism. In the U.S., she suggested establishing the New York Bureau of Immigration. "The government's policy regarding the immigrant had been negative, concerned with exclusion and deportation, with the head tax and the enforcement of treaties. By our laws we are protected from the pauper, the sick, and the vicious. The need for constructive social measures has long been indicated. The immigrant brings in a steady stream of new life and new blood to the nation."

Lillian was involved in Columbia University's establishment of a nursing program in 1910. In 1912, she was named as the first president of the National Organization for Public Health Nursing. In 1915, she published her most famous book that describes the founding of her key organization, The House on Henry Street. Through her writing, she shed light on the vital services provided by the organization and the impact it had on advancing social welfare and healthcare in impoverished communities.

By the 1920s, Lillian established nursing centers across New York to train nurses in public health and operated a maternity service. She eventually oversaw a public health corps of 260 nurses, who cared for 350,000 people a year. Lillian's influence in public health extended to a global reach. Henry Street nurses were serving in 48 countries across Europe, Asia, and Africa. She corresponded with suffragists from England and worked with peace activists to oppose WWI and war with Mexico and served as chair of the American Union Against Militarism. In 1919, she represented the Red Cross Nursing Service at the first international Health Conference, a precursor to the World Health Organization.

She traveled to the early Soviet Union and overlooked the problems of their government, writing: "New appeals take the place of the old religious commands, the extension of democracy through the enfranchisement of women, the plea for service to humanity through social work, stir the younger generation and give expression to a religious spirit."

In 1930, Lillian retired to Connecticut in poor health. 1934, She wrote Windows on Henry Street to discuss the connection between nursing, politics, and social reform. "The American development of nursing meant that spirit of consecration, the power of organization, the realization that the nurse is an effective and indispensable educator, and that her profession is of community importance."

Though Lillian died in 1940, the Henry Street Settlement is still open and operating, its mission honoring her legacy to better humanity: "We at Henry Street have become internationalists, because we have found that the problems of one set of people are the problems of all."

Emma Goldman

Emma Goldman was a nurse, anarchist, and activist who dedicated her life to freedom for all people. Her life and ideas are as radical today as they were a hundred years ago. Born June 27, 1869 to a Russian Jewish family, her autobiography reports that she was always rebellious and outspoken. At 17, she and her sister immigrated from St. Petersburg to live with their older sister in Rochester, New York. Emma had been working in a factory in St. Petersburg. She was not interested in a traditional woman's life, although she got married soon after immigrating.

Emma did not find the freedom in America she had hoped for and was dissatisfied with low paying factory work, a bad marriage, and poor living conditions. She saw the connection between personal discontent and the labor movement's fight against exploitation and terrible working conditions. At the time, laborers were striking for eight-hour workdays across the country. In 1886, the Chicago Haymarket riot began when police violently attacked laborers striking for an eight-hour workday. The confrontation escalated when someone threw a bomb at the police and killed eleven people including seven police officers. Eight anarchist labor leaders were arrested for the death of the police officers. Four were executed, although there was little evidence they were responsible.

Emma felt a profound connection with the anarchist leaders and was deeply inspired by their ideals. She came to see Anarchism as the solution to both her personal dissatisfaction and the broader social injustices she observed. Driven by this belief, she dedicated her life to advocating for a society based on principles of equality, mutual aid, and individual freedom. While modern anarchism is often associated with mayhem, to Emma it was a beautiful ideology dedicated to freedom, autonomy and cooperation. Anarchists worked to limit the destructive power of all forms of government. Anarchism was a political philosophy that went back hundreds of years and had inspired people such as Henry David Thoreau.

At the time, anarchism was a popular, international movement with widespread support. Emma later wrote in her book: "Anarchism stands for the liberation of the human mind from the dominion of religion and liberation of the human body from the coercion of property, liberation from the shackles and restraint of government. It stands for a social order based on the free grouping of individuals. Anarchism was the philosophy of a new social order based on liberty unrestricted by man-made law. The theory that all forms of government rest on violence, and therefore wrong and harmful as well as unnecessary. The liberation of the human mind from religion, from property, and restraint of government." For her, anarchism was both a political and a personal philosophy,:"I want freedom, the right to self-expression, everybody's right to beautiful, radical things."

At twenty, she left Rochester and moved to New York City with just a sewing machine, a few dollars and plans to change the world. She had the name of several anarchists to look up and quickly met two men who would impact the rest of her life: Alexander 'Sasha' Berkman, a Russian writer, and Johan Most, a German politician, speaker, and editor. Although she was terrified of public speaking, Most pushed her to do a speaking tour. She started organizing and attending the International Socialist Congress, while working up to 18 hours a day as a seamstress.

Her personal life was as radical and devoted to freedom as her political life. She openly practiced 'free love', being romantically and sexually involved with whomever she chose. She was determined to not have children and was an advocate for birth control. She was often alienated from others in the movement, who found her scandalous due to her outspoken support for free love, birth control, and feminism. These radical views, combined with her unapologetic advocacy for women's rights and personal freedoms, set her apart and led to controversy within the anarchist community.

Working closely with Sasha Berkman as her romantic and political partner, she organized boycotts and demonstrations. Sasha and Emma felt the use of violence was justified in their fight for freedom. Sasha was involved in an assassination attempt against Henry Clay Frick, anti-union chairman of the Carnegie Steel company. Berkman felt this assassination was justified after Frick was involved in the murder of laborers during the 1892 Homestead Strike against his company. Frick survived the attempted murder and Berkman was sentenced to jail for twenty-two years. Shortly after Sasha's sentencing, Emma was sent to prison for a year on Blackwell's Island for inciting a riot.

While incarcerated, Emma became ill and needed hospitalization. Towards the end of her month in the prison hospital, Dr. White, "a humane and kindly man", asked her to stay to take care of the sick due to nursing shortages. She discussed this time in her autobiography: "Dr. White, during his rounds, asked me if I would like to remain in the hospital and help out as a nurse, despite knowing nothing about nursing. I should indeed, but I know nothing about nursing: He replied that neither did anyone else in the prison. I could easily pick up the elementary things about tending the sick. He would teach me to take the pulse and temperature and to perform similar services."

The conditions were poor and she treated everything from infectious disease to childbirth. "It gave me the opportunity to come close to the sick women and bring a little cheer into their lives. I had so much to give; it was a joy to share with my sisters who had neither friends nor attention. I was gradually given the entire charge of the hospital ward. The prison had been the crucible that tested my faith. It helped me to discover strength in my own being, the strength to stand alone, the strength to live my life and fight for my ideals, against the whole world if need be."

In 1894, she was released and continued working as a nurse at Beth Israel Hospital in Manhattan. "I loved my profession, and I was able to earn more money than at any time previously. The joy of no longer having to grind at the machine, in or out of a shop was great; greater still the satisfaction of having more time for reading and public activity." She decided to pursue professional nursing and midwifery training in Vienna, at the Allgemeines Krankenhausm as there were few such professional schools in the U.S. "The A.K. gave courses on and treated every ill of the human body, offered splendid opportunities to the eager and willing student."

She returned to New York in 1896 to work as a nurse and as an activist. "Nursing provided me with an identity as a laborer, but without compromising my fundamental belief. It put me into intimate contact with the very people my ideal strove to help and emancipate. It brought me face to face with the living conditions of the workers, about which, until then, I had talked and written mostly from theory. Their squalid surroundings, the dull and inert submission to their lot, made me realize the colossal work yet to be done to bring about the change our movement was struggling to achieve."

As a midwife, she was distressed by the reproductive care available to poor women in New York. They had no access to contraception or legal abortion and were trying to raise their children without basic resources. She was impressed by the struggle of poor women against unwanted pregnancies and reported that most of them lived in continual dread of pregnancy. She was comfortable with taking care of mothers, sex workers, and women of all backgrounds: "I felt, however, that in my capacity as a nurse I could not concern myself with the particular trade or occupation of my patients. I had to minister to their physical needs. Besides, I was not only a nurse, I was also an anarchist who knew the social factors behind human action."

She clearly saw the connection between health, poverty, and policy choices long before this became widely accepted. In 1901, Emma began working as a nurse under an assumed name due to the widespread notoriety she gained following the assassination of President William McKinley by the young Polish anarchist, Leon Czolgosz. While she did not know him personally, Leon was inspired by Emma's work. Emma was arrested after she refused to denounce the murder, writing in The Tragedy at Buffalo, that his act was a response to the oppression of the working class. Although she was acquitted on these charges of inciting his violence, the case was widely publicized and brought her a great deal of notoriety and complicated her nursing work.

She left nursing in 1905 to help found the magazine *Mother Earth* and to spend more of her time promoting anarchism. "I was utterly exhausted and unable to face the ordeal of nursing. I had realized for some time past that I could not keep up much longer the hard work, responsibility, and anxiety my profession involved while continuing my platform activities."

In 1906, Sasha was released from prison and they were reunited. They spent ten years together, traveling and promoting anarchism and opposition to World War I. Emma opposed World War I because she viewed it as a capitalist conflict that exploited the working-class using nationalism and militarism. Emma and Sasha organized a No Conscription League and encouraged people to oppose the draft. This was seen as a direct challenge to the U.S. government's war efforts. They were arrested and charged with conspiracy to obstruct the draft under the Espionage Act of 1917 and sentenced to two years in prison. When Emma and Sasha were released from prison in 1919, they were deported to Russia and stripped of U.S. citizenship.

They arrived amid the Russian Revolution, during the civil war between the Bolsheviks (Reds) and the Counter revolutionaries (Whites). The revolution began in October 1917 when the Russian army overthrew the Tsar, and Vladimir Lenin returned to lead the Communist Bolsheviks, promising land reform and ending Russia's involvement in World War I. The Bolsheviks eventually defeated the other socialist factions and established the USSR in 1922.

Emma was initially a vocal supporter of the communist revolution, but was fearless in her criticism of the reality she saw once living in Russia. She spoke out against the oppressive and authoritarian government and poor living conditions of the people. At a time when many leftist radicals were fully supportive of the new government, she was determined to fight for true freedom. She was quickly at odds with the new communist government and was not allowed to work as a nurse, even though her skills were badly needed in the country. By 1921, Emma and Sasha were desperate to leave Russia. They were able to obtain travel visas to Germany and England but were not allowed to return to the United States.

For the last twenty years of her life, she did not have a home but continued to promote anarchism, equality and freedom. In her late 60s, she traveled to Spain during the Civil War there to support the anarchist- socialist coalition and their democratic, collective governments against General Franco, a fascist military leader backed by Hitler and Mussolini. Emma and Sasha aspired to witness the emergence of an improved form of government that embodied their ideals of freedom and justice. However, they were disappointed as they saw both the Spanish Republic and the Soviet Union fail to achieve these aspirations. Despite their hopes, these governments did not fulfill the promise of a fair and just society they had envisioned.

In 1936, Sasha, who had terminal cancer, committed suicide. Emma died in Canada four years later from a stroke. Although she had been banned from returning to the U.S. alive, she was buried next to the Haymarket Martyrs in Chicago. Emma Goldman epitomized the spirit of activism, intertwining her nursing career with her commitment to anarchism. She used her nursing wages to fund her revolutionary activities, which exposed her to the harsh realities faced by the working class. Despite the significant personal cost, she courageously spoke the truth and remained hopeful for a better future. Her writings, including an autobiography and numerous essays on anarchism, reflect her dedication to freedom as both a political stance and a personal conviction.

Adah Samuels Thoms

Early twentieth-century New York was teeming with activist nurses who frequently collaborated and supported one another. These nurses, driven by a shared commitment to social reform, advanced the nursing profession and played an important role in addressing social issues and advocating for improved healthcare and labor conditions. This list would not be complete without Adah Belle Samuels Thoms, a pioneering African American nurse and organizer.

She was born on January 12, 1870, in Richmond, Virginia during the hopeful reconstruction era after the Civil War. As an African American, Adah faced very limited opportunities in racially segregated Virginia in the era of Jim Crow laws. She moved to New York City to study at the Cooper Union Institute, later graduating from the Lincoln School for Black Nurses.

Adah Thoms, Mary Mahoney, and Martha M. Franklin created the National Association of Colored Graduate Nurses (NACGN) in 1908 to support Black graduate nurses and prove that Black nurses could meet the same professional standards as their white counterparts. The organization dissolved when the American Nurses Association finally integrated in the early 1950s.

As President of the NACGN from 1916 to 1923, Adah campaigned for Black nurses' acceptance into the American Red Cross and the United States Army Nurse Corps (USANC). During WWI, neither the American Red Cross nor the USANC would accept Black nurses. Adah and the NACGN convinced them to make an exception to this policy due to the nursing needs during the 1918 Spanish influenza epidemic. This integration was only temporary but helped move the needle.

Despite being desperate for medical personnel, the Army would not allow black nurses to join the USANC. About half of the 20,000 white nurses that enlisted worked in the U.S. to fill shortages at home. In response Adah organized and helped fund the Blue Circle Nurse Corps in 1917, creating a platform for Black nurses to work within their communities. It took twenty years of activism and WWII for the Army to allow Black nurses to enlist in the USANC. An initial quota of 56 Black nurses were allowed to join in 1940, with full integration in 1944. This fight is discussed in more detail in the book Nursing Civil Rights: Gender and Race in the Army Nurse Corps.

Adah was appointed to the Women's Advisory Council on Venereal Disease by the Assistant Surgeon General of the Army in 1921, at a time when very few African Americans served in federal advisory roles.

She retired from Lincoln Hospital in 1923 but continued working with the NACGN, writing Pathfinders: A History of the Progress of Colored Graduate Nurses in 1929. Thoms was active in religious and social reform movements, including the National Urban League and the NAACP to fight for justice for African Americans. She died in 1943 in New York City and was buried beside her husband, Henry Smith.

Harriet Boyd Hawes

Although her name is not well known, Harriet Boyd Hawes led a life as an adventurous real-life Indiana Jones. Born on October 11, 1871, in Boston, Massachusetts, she was a pioneering American archaeologist, nurse, relief worker, foreign correspondent, and professor.

As the youngest of five children and the only girl, Harriet faced early challenges when her mother passed away when she was less than a year old. She credited growing up with her brothers for making her tough and shared a deep love of the classics with her brother Alex. Harriet received an excellent education and pursued her passion for the classics at Prospect Hill School and Smith College, where she was drawn to the field of archaeology. Tragically, her brother Alex passed away during her final year in college. After earning her B.A. in 1892, Harriet taught Classics in North Carolina and Delaware.

When her father died in 1896, Harriet used part of her inheritance to go on a grand tour of Europe. She eventually chose to stay in Greece and began studying at the American School of Classical Studies in Athens, although she was excluded from many activities as a woman. While in Athens, she found herself in the middle of the Cretan rebellion and the start of the Greco-Turkish War. This conflict, centered on Crete, escalated when Greece annexed the island in defiance of international powers, sparking war with the Ottoman Empire.

Harriet, eager to contribute to the war effort, trained as a nurse. Although she initially failed an exam in front of Queen Olga of Greece, she didn't let this setback deter her. Determined to make a difference, she wrote to the queen, requesting permission to join the Red Cross. Her persistence paid off and she arrived at the Volos hospital in April 1897, ready to provide care and support to those in need. The town was overwhelmed with wounded Greek soldiers, and the conditions were terrible: overcrowded, working 24-hour shifts amid typhus outbreaks.

In addition to working as a nurse, she also was writing dispatches and serving as a war correspondent for the *Philadelphia Public Ledger* and the *New York Journal*. She wrote of the war: "These wounded Greeks certainly know how to bear pain. The candles and torches flared on their powder-grimed faces as they were jolted... but never a complaint did they utter. They would only follow you with dumb, pleading eyes that asked for everything where nothing could be given." As the Greek army retreated, Harriet walked 22 miles with the troops. Even after the war concluded with an Ottoman victory, she continued nursing the soldiers.

Following her recognition by The Greek Society of the Red Cross for her service, Harriet returned to the United States. In 1898, the Spanish American War started and Harriet again volunteered for the Red Cross, although the war ended before she made it to the front. Instead, she returned to Greece on a fellowship, a rare female archeologist and classicist.

In 1900, she joined British archeologists to start excavations in Heraklion, Crete at the palace of King Minos of Minoa. The Minoans were an early civilization from 3000 to 1000 B.C. that had an important influence on Greek civilization. This archeological site, the setting for the stories of Icarus and the Minotaur, eventually became one of the most famous in the world.

While she was excavating on Crete, Harriet traveled across Europe and Turkey and held a teaching position at Smith College where she received her M.A. (in 1901) and an honorary doctorate (in 1910). Harriet also traveled across the United States, volunteering at Chicago's Hull House, where she assisted Greek immigrants in settling into the city. It was there that she met Edith Hall, another pioneering American archaeologist.

Eventually, Harriet developed her own excavation site at Gournia on the island of Crete, unearthing a significant Minoan archaeological site. She documented her groundbreaking findings and conclusions in a book about Gournia. While working on these excavations, she used her nursing skills to provide care for her working crew. While in Crete, she met Charles Hawes, an English anthropologist, whom she married in 1906.

That same year they had their first child, Alexander. Henry and Harriet wrote a book, *Crete the Forerunner of Greece*, which describes the civilizations at Crete that laid the foundations of Greek classical civilization. While her husband worked as a professor, Harriet taught Greek, Latin and history while raising their two children.

She was a philanthropist and activist, fundraising for the Balkan War of 1912. In 1914, the assassination of Archduke Franz Ferdinand triggered World War I. Harriet advocated for the U.S. to join the war effort, and then joined as a volunteer. She left her husband and children (ages 9 and 5) to travel to Europe in December 1915, taking supplies with her. She eventually traveled to Brindisi, where she cared for Serbian refugees. By February, Harriet had obtained permission to travel to Corfu where 100,000 Serbian soldiers were stranded, starving, and suffering from typhus. She collaborated with French and Serbian doctors and nurses, providing critical medical care and support.

Harriet next worked to create the Smith College Relief Unit, composed of more than a dozen women from 14 different Smith classes. Included werephysicians, professors, and social workers who volunteered to perform civilian relief work. Harriet combined forces with Dr. Alice Weld Tallant, who served as the unit's medical director and provided medical care for people within a 30-mile radius of the village Grécourt. This story is novelized in Lauren Willig's book, *The Band of Sisters.*

Harriet worked with the relief unit, the YMCA, and the Red Cross in France for one year. She sailed home to America in June 1918 just before the end of the war. After returning home, Harriet continued to make significant contributions to both education and archaeology. She taught ancient art at Wellesley College, where she became a renowned expert on Cretan history and archaeology. Throughout her academic career, she authored multiple books on archaeology, sharing her groundbreaking work on Gournia and Crete.

Alongside her professional achievements, Harriet devoted herself to raising her family, balancing her roles as a mother and a scholar. Harriet spent the last part of her life involved in national politics, supporting the League of Nations, socialism and labor rights during the Great Depression.

She moved to D.C. in 1936 after her husband's retirement to support labor rights legislation. She wrote screen plays based on

Greek legends. In the 30s, her political work turned toward anti-fascism and pro-democracy, opposing U.S. support for Franco and the McCarthy Hearings.

Twenty years after she was last there, Harriet returned to Athens with her daughter to visit her son, who had also become an archaeologist. She was living in Prague with her daughter when Hitler invaded Czechoslovakia, staying to help Jews escape. She spent her 67th birthday in a German prison before she escaped and returned home. Back in the U.S., she met with Eleanor Roosevelt to warn her of the risk the Germans presented and advocated for the U.S. to join in the war. When she passed away in 1945, she was requesting permission to assist in the Grecian Civil War.

Sophia Duleep Singh

Sophia Duleep Singh's life story is singular, characterized by her activism and her multifaceted identity as both Sikh royalty and a product of British society. Despite being caught between two worlds, she managed to forge a distinctive role for herself, using her experiences to champion various social causes and nursing to carve out her own path and assert her place in history.

Princess Sophia Duleep Singh was born in 1876 in London. Her grandfather was Maharaja Ranjit Singh, the revered leader of the Sikh Kingdom of the Punjab in Northern India. During his life, the Maharajah's power allowed him to resist British colonialism from gaining control of his kingdom. After his death of natural causes at the age of 59, a bloody power struggle left his youngest son, Duleep, with his fifth wife, as his only living heir. Duleep was made Maharajah at age 5, and The British East India Company quickly took advantage of this vulnerability. The British defeated their army and planned to control Duleep as their puppet ruler.

His twenty-three-year-old mother, Jindan, refused to follow the colonial orders. The British retaliated by murdering his uncle and imprisoning his mother, leaving Duleep completely alone in the world. Within a year of Duleep becoming Maharajah, the British had taken over the Sikh kingdom, forcing Duleep to sign over his fortune and to leave the Punjab forever. The British also took the allegedly cursed symbol of the Sikhs, the Koh-i-noor diamond, and brought it to Queen Victoria, where it remains in royal possession to this day.

Duleep was sent away from the Punjab to be raised as a Christian Englishman with a Scottish family. He became a favorite of Queen Victoria and her children, growing up amidst the Royal family. Despite his great wealth and fame, these privileges could not heal the wounds of his incredible loss. As an adult he began to rebel against the royal family and the Empire. Duleep's first act of open rebellion was thwarted when he made a failed attempt to return to the Punjab.

Defying the royal family's expectations, he chose to marry Bamba Müller, a sixteen-year-old born to a German father and an Ethiopian mother, rather than someone selected by the royals. She was a Christian who had been abandoned by her parents to a religious cloister in Cairo. Duleep and Bamba settled at Elveden estate, where they had six children: Victor, Frederick, Bamba, Catherine, Sophia and Edward. Duleep spent lavishly and was a heavy drinker, eventually having his finances cut off by the Queen. Sophia and her sisters had a limited education and ran wild on the estate with little supervision from either parent.

Duleep converted back to Sikhism and made his second attempt to return to the Punjab, sailing from England with his entire family. They were stopped in Aden (now Yemen) by British authorities. With nowhere else to go, Bamba returned to England with the children, including 11-year-old Sophia. Their father was humiliated, refused to return to England, and publicly renounced any responsibility for his family.

One year later in England, Sophia contracted typhoid. While she recovered, her mother contracted the same illness and died at her bedside while caring for her. She and her siblings were essentially orphaned, although Queen Victoria arranged for their financial support and residences at Hampton Court. Her father lived aimlessly in Europe, drinking heavily, remarrying and having two more daughters before dying in Paris in 1893. Tragedy continued to stalk the family when Sophie's youngest brother, Eddie died of tuberculosis at age 13 with his sisters by his side.

Sophia, unlike her older sisters who openly hated the court, debuted into British society. While her brother received education at Cambridge, the sisters had limited options for education or marriage. Her sister Catherine spent most of her life living with her partner and former governess, Lina Schaeffer, in Germany. Her sister Bamba traveled to America to enter medical school, although was unable to complete school when all the female students were expelled.

After the death of Queen Victoria in 1901, Bamba, Catherine and Sophia were able to travel to India for the first time (her brothers were not allowed anywhere near the country). They traveled to Delhi and then to Lahore, warmly greeted by Sikhs, but shunned by the British colonials. Her sister, Bamba, decided to stay in India, while Sophia returned to England where she enjoyed cycling and raising dogs.

After several aimless years, Sophia became politically involved in the fight for Indian and women's rights. She fought for better treatment of the Lascars, immigrant servant Indians living in England. She also became involved with the suffragette movement for women's voting rights. She dedicated her time and money to the Women's Social and Political Union, a militant women's rights political organization. Sophia protested and was arrested in this fight. Women didn't gain full suffrage until 1928.

In 1906, Sophia returned to India to visit Bamba, joining in the fight for Indian independence and the creation of the Indian

National Congress. During her visit, Sophia was profoundly inspired by the activism of Lala Lajpat Rai, a prominent leader in India's independence movement. In 1910, King Edward died, and the Duleep Singh family lost their personal connection to the British Royal Family.

In the beginning of World War I, 40,000 Indian troops were deployed to fight for the UK. Wounded Indian soldiers were sent back to England to segregated hospitals set up for Muslim, Hindu and Sikh soldiers. Although racism barred English women from serving as nurses to the Indian soldiers, The Lady Hardinge Hospital was run by nurse Edith McCall Anderson and staffed by volunteer nurses who had grown up in colonial India and spoke Hindi. Sophia, who could not speak Hindi, volunteered as a Red Cross nurse. She was treated as royalty by Punjabi soldiers who were in awe of the granddaughter of Ranjit Singh. She organized India Day as a fundraising effort for the soldiers while the government desperately tried to hide her family connections.

By 1919 and the end of World War I, Sophia was able to reunite with her sisters as the fight for Indian independence gained momentum. Gandhi, partially inspired by the work of the suffragettes in London, had returned to India from South Africa. That same year, the massacre at Jallianwala Bagh in Amritsar, the capital of the Sikh kingdom, where British troops killed hundreds of peaceful protesters, intensified resistance to British colonialism.

Determined to contribute to the growing independence movement, Sophia traveled to Lahore to be with her sister. Together, they journeyed across the Sikh kingdom, adopting traditional dress to blend in. Despite their efforts to evade them, British guards followed them everywhere, but this did not deter Sophia and her sister from their mission to support the cause.

As they fought for the future of their homeland, their family line came to an end. Her brothers, Victor and Freddie, both died childless. Catherine came to live with Sophia in England after the death of her partner, Lina. Sophia lived in the English countryside with her trusted friend and housekeeper, Bosie, and Bosie's husband and daughter.

During World War II, the family took in child refugees from London who were fleeing the city to escape the devastating German bombs. Sophia lived to see the end of World War II and the independence of India from Britain. However, this independence came at a significant cost, with the partition of the Punjab dividing the Sikhs between India and Pakistan. It is estimated that ten million people were displaced, and hundreds of thousands were killed in the ensuing violence between Hindus, Muslims, and Sikhs. Sophia died on August 22, 1948, in her sleep with Bosie at her side. Although she was a Christian, she wanted to be cremated in the Sikh custom. Her only surviving sibling Bamba scattered her ashes in India.

Sophia's life and activism was unique and forged out of the terrible treatment of her people and her family by the British Empire. She was rendered largely powerless as a woman and a Sikh in British society, but fought for what she could, for the rights of women, and her fellow Sikhs and Indians.

Elena Arizmendi Mejía

Elena Arizmendi Mejía was many things: nurse, Mexican revolutionary, muse, and feminist activist. Elena was born in Mexico City on January 18, 1884, to Jesús Arizmendi and Isabel Mejía. Her maternal grandfather was Maj. Gen. Ignacio Mejía, the minister of war and navy under President Benito Juárez. Elena spent part of her childhood in Oaxaca, living with her grandfather, before returning to Mexico City at age eight. Her stable family life ended abruptly in 1898 when her mother died during childbirth. At only fourteen, Elena assumed responsibility for managing the household and raising her five younger brothers.

Her father remarried in 1900, and Elena, at age 16, married Francisco Carreto later that year. Elena and Francisco had a son, Francisco Tiburcio, who tragically died in infancy, and Elena was left infertile. Likely due to her wealth and family connections, she was able to get a rare divorce, leaving her abusive husband to start her life over in Mexico City.

In 1909, at age 25, she enrolled in nursing school at Santa Rosa Hospital in San Antonio, Texas, using her inheritance to pay for school. Professional nursing was still new in Mexico, with the first general hospital built in 1905 and the first nursing school established in 1907. Elena studied in San Antonio for three years, living in a religious order. She would have taken twenty required courses during her three years and spent 12 hours a day, 6 days a week studying and working in the hospital. The school provided charity care to migrant workers and emphasized obedience and compliance.

While in San Antonio, Elena formed a close friendship with Francisco and Sara Madero, who were living in exile due to their opposition to the presidency of Porfirio Díaz. Madero's revolutionary ideals deeply resonated with Elena, and she started supporting the revolution through propaganda and fundraising.

The Mexican revolution officially started in 1910 after Porfirio Diaz, who had been president for 31 years, refused to step down at age 81. Socialists and leftists, including Emiliano Zapata, Pancho Villa, Madero, Pascual Orozco and Alberto Obregon, joined together in revolt against Diaz and his regime. Madero wrote the *Plan of San Luis Potosi*, which outlined how to transform Mexico, including indigenous rights and social, economic, and land reform.

In 1911, just days before her graduation, Elena left nursing school and boarded a train back to Mexico City. Upon her return, Elena became frustrated with the Mexican Red Cross, which refused to provide aid to revolutionaries. She wrote an open letter to Luz González Cosío Acosta de López, the president of the Mexican Red Cross, demanding that the organization extend its services to all wounded, regardless of political affiliation.

When her appeal was denied, Elena and her brother Carlos founded La Cruz Blanca Neutral (The Neutral White Cross) on May 5, 1911. Drawing on the principles of the Geneva Convention of 1864, the Cruz Blanca Neutral aimed to "render its human services to all those who suffer, without distinction of political parties, religion, or nationality, caring for all with the same piety and solicitude." Elena organized medical students and nurses, raised funds, and opened a field hospital in Ciudad Juárez.

By the end of the year, the organization had expanded to include twenty-five branches across Mexico. Her efforts earned her widespread recognition, including a gold medal from the Gran Liga Obrera for her dedication to aiding the wounded. In addition to her humanitarian work, Elena was elected as the first female partner of the Sociedad Mexicana de Geografía y Estadística (Geographic and Statistical Society of Mexico).

Soon after Cruz Blanca split into two parts: The Cruz Blanca Mexicana, headed by Elena and Sarah Maduro and the Cruz Blanca Neutral, headed by the medical students. The split was acrimonious with the groups fighting over the focus of their efforts and over Elena's posing with bandoliers for publicity photographs.

That year, the revolution appeared to be a success with Diaz going into exile and Madero elected president. Elena also began her relationship with Jose Vasconcelos, a married writer, lawyer, and secretary of education in Madero's cabinet. The vision of the revolution did not last long. Madero was assassinated in a U.S. supported coup after serving as president for less than two years. The coalition that had built the revolution fell apart. Emilio Zapata and other radicals wanted widespread land reform and equality but were shut out by the more conservative revolutionaries. While a new Constitution was written in 1917, a succession of revolutionary generals were elected president, but none held power for very long. Within this power vacuum, the Institutional Revolution Party, or PRI, was founded and went on to dominate Mexico for 71 years.

Elena and Jose went into exile in 1915, settling first in San Antonio, where Vasconcelos split his time between his family and Elena, and then moved together to Manhattan. Elena's life in New York was exciting, as she was connected to the Hispanic cultural elite, but her relationship with Vasconcelos was difficult. He opposed her independence and literary, feminist, and artistic efforts. They broke up in 1916. In his books *La Tormenta* and *Ulises Criollo*, Vasconcelos based his character: "Adriana", one of the most famous femme fatales in Mexican literature, on Elena.

Elena briefly married Robert Duerch, an American businessman, but they divorced quickly. Elena wrote: "Divorce seems to me an empty form given the way I feel, I will not have another husband." She decided to stay in New York and build her own life among the bohemian and artistic culture of Greenwich Village. She interacted with Hispanic rights activists and communist revolutionaries such as John Reed and Louise Bryant.

Later in her life, Elena poured her efforts into feminism and Latin American suffrage. White attending the Congress of Pan American Women in 1922, she helped form the League of Iberian and Hispano American Women. The League was created to provide equality for Spanish speaking women and to create a Hispanic feminist culture that stood separate from American efforts. She worked as a journalist and founded a feminist magazine, *Feministo Internacional*, and a union, Mujeres de la Raza in 1923. She was involved in La Liga de la Raza, a league of Hispanic journalists and writers who focused on modern Hispanic feminism and culture. Elena published an autobiography, *La Vida Incompleta*, to tell her story and separate herself from Vasconcelos' portrayal of her as a jezebel like character.

Elena returned home to Mexico in 1936 for the 25th anniversary of the White Cross, working with the organization until her death in 1949. She did not live to see Mexican women earn the right to vote, which didn't become law until 1953.

Nella Larson

Nella Larsen became one of the great writers of the Harlem Renaissance while working as a nurse and librarian. She was not a political activist but wrote critically on themes of racial and gender identity in early 20th century America. Her life story opens a window into the progressive institutions of 1920s New York and how both public health and public library systems benefited the lives of all the city's citizens.

Nellie Walker was born in Chicago in 1891 to a Danish immigrant mother and an Afro-Caribbean father from the Dutch West Indies. Nella grew up in Chicago when it was just 1% Black, before the great migration of African Americans from the South. Her early life was marked by the disappearance of her father when she was two and her mother's remarriage to a White Danish immigrant. As she grew up, Chicago became increasingly segregated. Nella was isolated within a Scandinavian immigrant community, separated from African American culture and neighborhoods.

At 18, Nella decided to attend Fisk, a historically Black university in Nashville, Tennessee, as many of the colleges in the U.S. would have been segregated and off limits for her. She struggled at school and was expelled her first year, her biographer speculating that it was for violating strict dress codes. Nella would rebel against strict, hierarchical organizations for much of her life.

After her expulsion, Nella traveled to live with her mother's family in Copenhagen for four years. She attended college courses while in Denmark but did not finish a degree. At 21, she moved to New York to study nursing at the Lincoln Hospital and Home in the Bronx. Lincoln Hospital was a unique, semi-integrated institution. It had been founded in 1839 by white women as a charity home for elderly, poor African Americans and was later expanded to a hospital that primarily served Jewish patients. The staff was segregated; all the physicians were white males, and the nursing staff and school were black females. The nursing school was one of the best in the country at a time when nursing education was still largely unregulated and not yet professionalized. The hospital was staffed with nurse trainees, who were contracted out by the hospital to earn income as private nurses. Nella lived inside the hospital in a room with 12 other women.

Her three-year nursing course was progressive, starting with three months in housekeeping, then working for several months in different wards: pediatric, surgical, emergency, gynecology, obstetrics, and infectious disease. The student nurses had a heavy academic course load in addition to twelve hour shifts six days a week and mandatory church services. They were only allowed a half-day break on Sundays and were paid six dollars a month, with free room, board, and tuition. Larsen was a little older than the other students but enjoyed living in the city.

Upon graduating, she took a position as head nurse of a ward at the Lincoln Hospital. She was quickly promoted to serve as Assistant Superintendent of the Nurse Training School, working under Adah Thoms, the nursing pioneer who helped found the National Association of Colored Graduate Nurses, and worked to integrate the U.S. Army Corps.

Nella briefly left New York to work at the Tuskegee Institute in Alabama. Tuskegee was founded by Booker T. Washington in

1881 to provide technical and practical education to African Americans. It is still in operation and was a highly regarded hospital entirely run by African Americans. While Tuskegee is often associated with the horrific syphilis experiments, it is an important institution that prioritized African American health care. Nella was appointed as head nurse of the Institute, working 14-hour days as a teacher, supervisor, and nurse at the 53-bed hospital. Tuskegee was not a good fit for her, as it was very strictly run and required a high level of obedience and conformity of all its employees. Nella was never a conformist and wrote later about being at odds with Southern culture.

After Tuskegee, she returned to New York to again work as Assistant Superintendent at Lincoln, teaching pharmacology and nursing history. She worked with Adah on integrating the American Red Cross. She left the hospital to take a position as a public health nurse in the Bureau of Preventable Diseases in the New York City Health Department. She was assigned to work as a nurse in the primarily white, affluent Bronx. Her nursing work included public health education, hygiene enforcement, and investigating infectious diseases, especially typhoid and measles. This role was powerful and independent, as she could legally force someone with certain diseases into quarantine.

The New York Health Department was a revolutionary public health institution, with emphasis on wellness, prevention, and education, and had legal restrictions against racial discrimination. Although challenging, the work provided a good salary and career opportunities, and Nella made enough to be able to live on her own. She was working as a public health nurse during the 1918 Spanish Influenza epidemic that eventually killed 675,000 Americans. Larsen was involved in the planning and organizing of the community response. By the end of the epidemic more than 500,000 people (of

5.5 million) in New York had been infected. The epidemic continued through 1919, but not a single Bureau Nurse died, because of their masking and careful infection control.

During these years, Larsen became romantically involved with Dr. Elmer Imes, one of the only African American men in the U.S. with a PhD in Physics. They married on May 3, 1919, and settled in Harlem, just as the Harlem Renaissance and African American literary and artistic culture flourished. The period helped inspire the Civil Rights movement and was an essential moment of American cultural history.

Nella started her writing career for the Brownies Book, the children's magazine of the National Association for the Advancement of Colored People (NAACP).

Nella also became active in the New York Public Library at 135th Street. Headed by the librarian Ernestine Rose, the library was a center of a diverse Black cultural community that included integrationists, separatist supporters of Marcus Garvey, and socialists. While Nella was still working as a public health nurse, she planned an art exhibit and attended the New York Public Library school.

She left nursing to work in the NYPL Children's Department in the Lower East Side, a neighborhood filled with Russian Jewish refugees. She interacted with the literary elite of both Harlem and Greenwich Village, including literary greats such as Langston Hughes, Eugene O'Neil and Edna St. Vincent Millay.

In 1926, Nella published her first story, *The Wrong Man*, in Forum Magazine and quit her job to start writing full time. She loved the busy cultural and social life of Harlem. She wrote her first two novels, *Quicksand* (1928) and *Passing* (1929). Both novels explore the experiences of African American women in dealing with racism and feminism, outsider identities of being mixed race and non-Southern, and race and gender as performance. *Passing* was critically and commercially successful and was adapted into a movie in 2021.

She did not make enough money to support herself from her writing, and had to return to work at the library, living separately from her husband who took a teaching position at Fisk in Tennessee.

The next few years of her life were very challenging. She was accused of plagiarism for her short story, *Sanctuary,* while she learned that Elmer was having an affair with a woman in Nashville. She was offered a teaching position at Fisk, but did not want to leave New York. Instead, she and Elmer decided to have an open relationship.

In 1930, she was one of the first African Americans to win a prestigious Guggenheim Fellowship. She decided to use her fellowship earnings to travel to Spain and Portugal and write her next novel. She had to flee to France to escape the Spanish Civil War, returning to New York in the middle of the Depression. Nella and Elmer divorced soon after she returned and she did not report his affair, as it would have gotten Elmer fired, and she depended upon his salary of $150 a month to survive. Elmer did not live long after their divorce, dying of throat cancer in 1941.

After her divorce and return to New York, Nella withdrew from her previous social and cultural life. She stopped writing and returned to nursing. She worked with poor immigrant patients at Gouverneur's Hospital in the Lower East Side for seventeen years, eventually being promoted to chief nurse. She was well liked, although none of her co-workers knew of her past literary fame. She rebuilt her life with a new group of friends and contacted her mother and sister, who lived in L.A. Neither of them publicly acknowledged Nella or that they had a mixed-race family member.

After the city closed Gouverneur Hospital, she was hired as a night supervisor at the psychiatric unit at the Metropolitan Hospital, lying about her age so she wouldn't be forced to retire. Nella died of a heart attack in 1964 at the age of 73.

While Nella's fame as a writer and contributor to African American literary history overshadows her work as a nurse, nursing was still an integral part of her legacy. Both her literature and her involvement with two great progressive institutions of New York City demonstrated different radical approaches to life.

Vera Brittain

Like Florence Nightingale, Vera was born in Victorian England into a wealthy family and chose the nursing profession rather than early marriage. Nightingale died while Vera was still a teenager but their experiences as nurses during wartime shaped the course of their lives. While Vera did not have a strong impact within the profession of nursing like Nightingale, her memoir, *A Testament of Youth*, had a broad influence on the British public's perceptions of war, the role of women, and anti-war activism.

Vera was born in 1893 and, along with her very close brother Edward, was mostly raised by a governess. As a child, she was outspoken and bookish, writing from a very young age. After finishing school and debuting into society at 18, she fought to go to college instead of getting married. She enrolled at Somerville College, one of only two women's colleges at Oxford University. Vera's matriculation at Oxford coincided with the beginning of World War I. An entire generation of young British men enlisted, including her brother Edward and her fiancé poet Roland Leighton.

Vera wanted to contribute to the war effort and decided to volunteer for six months as a nurse. She joined the Voluntary Aid Detachment training at a hospital near her home. The destruction of her world began when Roland was killed by a sniper. Just a short time later, Edward was one of the one million men injured during the five-month battle of the Somme and was sent home to recover.

Vera decided to leave England to work as a war nurse, sailing to Italy and Malta to work at St. George's Hospital. While working long days in the hospital, more personal tragedy struck two of her close friends. Victor Richardson had been blinded and Geoffrey Thurlow had been killed. She decided to head home, leaving Malta just in time to see her brother head back to the front. She planned to marry Victor and serve as his caregiver, but he died before this could happen.

Despite these tragedies, Vera again returned to nursing, transferring to a British Army hospital camp on the front lines in France. She worked in Ward 29, treating German soldiers and victims of mustard gas. This experience led her to question the senselessness of war, as she wrote to her brother: "It is very strange that I should be nursing Hun prisoners, and it does show how absurd the whole thing is.... a dying man has no nationality."

She returned home to care for her ill mother and was at home when the family received news her brother had been killed in Italy. She wrote in her book, the *Testament of Youth*: "I was no longer capable of either enthusiasm or fear. Once an ecstatic idealist [...], I had now passed - like the rest of my contemporaries who had survived thus far - into a permanent state of numb disillusion. Whatever part of my brief adulthood I chose to look back upon — the restless pre-War months at home, the naïve activities of a college student, the tutelage to horror and death as a V.A.D. nurse, the ever-deepening night of fear and suspense and agony in a provincial town, in a university city, in London, in the Mediterranean, in France — it all seemed to have meant one thing, and one thing only, a striving, and a striving, and an ending in nothing. Now there were no more disasters to dread, and no friends left to wait for; with the ending of apprehension had come a deep, nullifying blankness, a sense of walking in a thick mist which hid all sights and muffled all sounds. I had no further experience to gain from the War; nothing remained except to endure it."

Having broken multiple nursing contracts, Vera was not able to return to the front line and she finished the war working at hospitals in London. In 1919, at the age of 25, Vera finished her history degree at Somerville. After graduating ,she started a career in journalism and was a supporter of the League of Nations, the precursor to the United Nations that hoped to promote cooperation between countries instead of war.

In 1923, she published her first novel, *The Dark Tide*, and married political scientist George Catlin. They later had two children. The trauma from the war continued to bring tragedy, as her father committed suicide in 1925 over grief from the loss of his son. Her second book was her memoir of the war, *A Testament of Youth* published in 1933. The memoir tells the story of her experience, the death and lives of so many men that she cared about. It also discusses war from an explicitly feminist viewpoint, of a woman rejecting a heroic narrative of war and being honest about the costs of war. The book was an instant bestseller and received widespread praise from critics like Virginia Woolf and Rebecca West.

Her activism continued into the next World War, where her pacifism brought her a great deal of public scorn and criticism. She spoke out against the bombing of German cities and campaigned for food relief, volunteering as a fire warden during the London bombings. She signed the Peace Pledge Union, agreeing that "War is a crime against humanity. I renounce war and am therefore determined not to support any kind of war. I am also determined to work for the removal of all causes of war."

She eventually wrote twelve books, including a sequel to *Testament of Youth, Testament of Experience* in which she wrote: "Didn't women have their war as well? They weren't, as these men make them, only suffering wives and mothers, or callous parasites, or mercenary prostitutes."

She continued her activism throughout her entire life, writing for pacifist magazines opposing apartheid, colonialism and nuclear proliferation. Vera died at age 76 in 1970 and was buried near her brother Edward's grave in Northern Italy.

Her years of nursing and her personal losses forged Vera into a pacifist and activist, far removed from the upper-class world she had been born into. She continues to inspire both feminist resistance and pacifism to this day. In 2014, a film, *Testament to Youth* was released, bringing her story to an even wider audience. Her daughter continued her work, protesting Britain's involvement in the 2003 Iraq War.

Susie Walking Bear Yellowtail

As one of the first Native American registered nurses, Susie Walking Bear Yellowtail broke barriers and dedicated her life to improving healthcare for Native American communities, advocating for better medical services and cultural understanding in healthcare practices.

Susie was born in 1903 in Pryor, Montana. Her father, an Apsáalooke Crow died when she was an infant. She was raised by her mother, an Ogalala Sioux, until she was orphaned at age 12. Susie initially attended a Catholic boarding school on the Crow reservation, although her mother took her out for fear of sexual abuse at the school.

Susie left the reservation at the age of 16 to attend the Bacone Indian School in Oklahoma, a training institution for Native students aimed at preparing them for service work. Her time there was part of the painful history of U.S. Indian Boarding Schools, where Native children were removed from their families to assimilate them into Euro-American culture, often resulting in significant cultural loss and trauma.

After a brief time in Oklahoma, her guardian paid for her to attend Northfield Seminary in Massachusetts. Susie worked as a housemaid and babysitter to earn her room and board. She was not treated well by her employer and left to start nursing school at Franklin County Memorial Hospital in Greenfield, MA, and the Boston City Hospital School of Nursing. She graduated in 1927, one of the first Native American Registered Nurses in the U.S.

Upon graduating, Susie joined the Indian Health Service, beginning her career at the Fond Du Lac Indian Hospital in Minnesota, where she worked with the Ojibwe people. After gaining experience working with other tribes for a few years, Susie returned to the Crow Reservation. Susie's work at the government-run Crow Agency hospital revealed the systemic issues plaguing Indian Health Service facilities.

Established by the U.S. government in 1868 to serve the Crow Indian Reservation, the agency's hospitals were marked by deplorable conditions and staffed largely by white medical professionals who failed to understand or respect their Native patients. Susie recalled confronting doctors, saying: "Just because we are Indians, doesn't mean you can do this to us. You think you can get away with it, but finally, somebody is here who knows what is going on." In her role, Susie assisted women in childbirth and advocated fiercely for better treatment and cultural competency in health care.

She resigned from the Crow Hospital when she married Thomas Yellowtail and settled with him on their ranch. In 1930, she had their first child, refusing to give birth in the reservation hospital. During the birth of her second child, she almost died due to the doctor's negligence at the Crow Hospital. She delivered her third child at home with a Crow midwife, Mary Takes the Gun, who incorporated indigenous practices during her labor. She had complications after this birth and had to return to the Crow Hospital, where she was sterilized without her consent during emergency surgery. This was a very common practice, encouraged by eugenicists throughout Native communities in the 1920s and 1930s. Her outspokenness and advocacy made it hard for her to find health care employment on the reservation.

In 1933, John Collier became the Commissioner of Indian Affairs and started reforms to improve conditions for Native communities. Around the same time, Susie's brother-in-law, Robert Yellowtail, was appointed head of the Crow Agency, where he worked to address systemic issues and advocate for the Crow people. For the first time, the all-male tribal council was allowed to file formal complaints against physicians and hospital staff, moving toward accountability. During this period, the Crow Health Council was established and the Crow Indian Women's Club began pushing for significant improvements, including the construction of a new hospital and the hiring of more Crow and Native nurses. Susie embraced her cultural identity more fully, adopting Crow dress and incorporating traditional healing practices into her nursing. She worked as a midwife both in homes and hospitals, providing essential maternal care to Crow families throughout the Little Bighorn Valley, often collaborating with another community midwife, Matilda Roundface.

In addition to her work as a nurse and midwife, Susie became a vocal activist, particularly against the forced sterilization of Native women, a practice that had devastating effects on communities throughout the U.S.

Her personal and professional experiences were fundamental to her role as an activist and nurse, allowing her to work as a patient advocate and monitor the quality of care within the IHS systems. One of her highest priorities was reproductive autonomy of indigenous women. The treatment she had suffered in the Crow Hospital was not unique but could be found at Indian hospital systems throughout the country.

In the early 1960s, she helped found the Native American Nurses Association. In addition to her work in health care and activism, Susie was a talented artist and American Indian Goodwill Ambassador, traveling to several foreign nations to promote understanding and appreciation of Native American heritage. As a member of the Crow Indian Ceremonial Dancers, Susie toured Europe and spent a month in Paris sharing Apsáalooke culture with an international audience. She was also a master beadwork artist.

At home, Susie remained deeply involved in her community, serving on both the Crow health and education committees. In 1961, President Kennedy appointed her to the Surgeon General's Advisory Committee on Indian Health. For thirty years she traveled across the country documenting problems in the Indian Health Service (IHS), including inadequate care, lack of resources, poor sanitation, and lack of linguistic and culturally appropriate care. She served in this role for three presidents, visiting Native Health centers throughout the country and advising the federal government on needed improvements.

Susie continued to be a community and national activist until she died in 1981. The mother, grandmother, nurse, midwife, and activist dedicated much of her life to improving the health and well-being of her community, and especially of Crow women and children. She helped to lead a national movement for Indigenous self-determination and sovereignty.

Irena Sendler

&

Ala Golab-Grynburg

There are several well-known stories of people who risked their lives to save Jews during the holocaust. Less well known is the story of Irena Sendler and Ala Golab-Grynburg, who were responsible for saving thousands of children from the Warsaw Ghetto. Irena survived the war and it is through her story we also know about Ala, who did not survive.

Irena Sendler was born Irena Stanislawa Krzyzanowskoa into a Catholic family in Otock, Poland. The town was very diverse, and she grew up speaking Yiddish with her Jewish neighbors. Her father was a socialist physician who died treating patients with typhus when she was still a child. His moral example left a great impact on her life. In 1927 Irena studied at the University of Warsaw and married a fellow Catholic, Mietek Sendler.

Her marriage did not last long, but they could not legally divorce, and Irena became involved with Jewish Adam Celnkier and joined his group of Jewish leftists, socialists, and bohemians. It was here that Irena met Ala Golab a married Jewish nurse from a well-known theatre family in Warsaw, although we know less about her life before the war.

After Irena graduated, she started working for the City of Warsaw in the Department of Social Welfare and Public Health as a public health nurse. She also studied at the Polish Free University with Dr. Helen Radlinksa, a remarkable social scientist and community organizer.

On September 1, 1939, Germany declared war on Poland. Both Adam and Irena's husband Mietek were called up for military service. Irena and her colleagues worked to help the refugees who flooded into Warsaw, causing a shortage of food, water and basic supplies. Less than a month later, 100,000 people had been killed and Warsaw surrendered to the German Army. At the time of invasion, Warsaw was home to a million people. One third were members of the Jewish community with a thousand-year history in the city.

Within two weeks, Germans segregated the city, establishing a Jewish ghetto. As the Gestapo ruthlessly worked to destroy the resistance, Irena, Adam and Dr. Radlinska formed an underground cell forging documents so that thousands of Jews could access public services. On November 16, 1940, the SS sealed the ghetto, locking Adam and the other Jewish residents in. Despite widespread starvation, the Germans continued shipping Jewish refugees from throughout Poland to the ghetto, increasing the population to 500,000.

Irena and her friend Ala, the chief nurse of the ghetto, worked to control typhus and other infections in the overcrowded conditions. Irena obtained a pass through the Department of Health to work inside the ghetto, risking execution to smuggle in typhus vaccines and food.

Working alongside Dr. Radlinksa's underground cell, Irena secured fake identities for Jewish children, often using the names of Christian children who had died. A priest gave them blank birth certificates after his church records were destroyed in a fire. They would smuggle children through the ghetto's walls and sewers, through emergency shelters in people's apartments, and on to catholic orphanages and rural convents. They carefully recorded the children's locations in the hopes of reuniting them with their families after the war.

In summer 1942, the first concentration camps opened. Irena smuggled Ala's 6-year-old daughter, Rami, to safety. On the day deportations began, Ala and a colleague Nacham Remba, set up a medical clinic to help divert some of those marked for transport. Over the course of several weeks, they saved a few hundred of the 300,000 transported. By the end of the summer, when the ghetto was nearly empty, the SS came to the hospital and began to execute all the Jewish patients who could not move. Some of the nurses and doctors took cyanide along with their families rather than face deportation. During this raid, Ala organized an escape with 30 children with trainee nurses carrying 2-3 infants each through the kitchen on a vegetable truck.

By this time, 85% of the 500,000 Jews in the ghetto had been deported, with another 60,000 either in slave labor or in hiding. Ala went to work in a ghetto factory, still working with Irena to smuggle out children. Another resistance cell, run by Aleksandra Dargielowa, using the code name Zegota, saved more than five hundred children through the Central Welfare Council.

The SS came to transport a Ghetto orphanage run by Dr. Janusz Korzack, a Jewish doctor and children's book author. As the orphans were loaded onto trains, Irena and Ala watched as he and his staff accompanied 200 children to their deaths at Treblinka. Irena tried desperately to convince Ala to escape the ghetto, even providing her fake identity papers. Like Dr. Korzack, Ala refused to save herself, instead sacrificing herself while her husband Alek was fighting for the resistance outside the city. Irena did convince her partner Adam and his mother to escape the ghetto, providing them with forged paperwork.

As the Gestapo grew suspicious of the welfare office, their director was sent to Auschwitz and much of their work was destroyed. Irena assumed leadership of the Child Welfare Division of Zegota and took on the code name Jolenta. By January 1943, the Germans started a final mass deportation of the ghetto but underestimated the Jewish resistance.

In August 1944, the Jews engaged in a 4-week armed uprising, the largest act of Jewish resistance in WWII. During the uprising, 13,000 Jews were killed, choosing to fight and die rather than be shipped to concentration camps. Ala was living in the ruins of the hospital. She and Nachum Remba established emergency medical stations for the fighters. While the Germans invaded the ghetto and started bombing, Irena and other Christians were no longer allowed to enter. Instead, they helped direct refugees who used the fighting as a cover to escape the ghetto. Ala was captured, hiding with her hospital team, and was loaded on train cars for transportation. The uprising ended in May 1943 when the SS demolished the Synagogue of Warsaw and sent the remaining 50,000 residents to concentration camps.

Ala was sent to a 15,000-person labor camp on the train route to Treblinka. While at the labor camp, she organized the resistance and operated a secret medical clinic. Ala and her network smuggled in weapons and planned an uprising and a prison escape, which started when the guards began executing prisoners during a roll call. The prisoners barricaded themselves in their barracks, which were set on fire, killing Ala and all the other fighters. Her husband and her daughter remained free in hiding.

In October 1943, Irena was denounced, arrested, and brought to Pawiak prison, where she was beaten and tortured. While the Gestapo knew that she was a part of the resistance, they had no idea of how important she was and did not find her list of hidden children. Many of the members of Irena's circle of resistance fighters were arrested and killed, but they did not betray those they had saved.

On January 20, 1944, Irena was scheduled for execution. The Gestapo even announced her death. But Zegota had bribed a German who allowed her to escape. Irena was instead free and hiding under a fake identity, Klara Dabrowska. Towards the end of the war, as the Soviet Army came closer to Warsaw, Irena reburied her list of 2500 Jewish children.

The Polish resistance planned an uprising for August 1944, hoping to defeat a weakened German Army with Soviet support. The Soviet help never arrived. Instead the German army destroyed the entire city in revenge. By the time Irena and Adam fled the city, six million Poles, including three million Jews, had been killed. In March, Irena and Adam returned to marry and help rebuild Warsaw. They had two children, a boy and a girl. Irena worked as the director of city welfare services and adopted two Jewish orphans. Irena and her friends dug up the list of children's names, which is now archived in Israel.

Ala's daughter, Rami Golab-Grynberg, was raised by her uncle and went on to become a nurse, with surviving descendants today. Irena, Ala, and their network of about 25 people saved 2500 children's lives. Irena lived to be 98 years old, passing away in 2008. A television movie, *The Courageous Heart of Irene Sendler*, was made in 2009.

Margaret Charles Smith

Margaret Charles Smith was one of the last of the "Granny Midwives" - Southern Black women who had been working as midwives for several hundred years, a tradition that has been nearly extinguished. Margaret's story was recorded because of interviews she did with Linda Janet Holmes for a book and a documentary, Miss Margaret - the story of an Alabama Granny Midwife.

Margaret was born in 1906, in Green County, Alabama, 75 miles from Birmingham. Green County was home to about 10,000 people, 80% African American, with a long history of plantation slavery, racism, and inequality. Nearby, one of the founders of gynecology, Dr. Marian Sims, practiced surgeries on the enslaved without anesthesia or consent. Alabama was also home to the Tuskegee Institute, a historically black university and center of the American black medical tradition.

During Margaret's life, people in Green County largely relied on traditional healers and midwives, who were well regarded in their community. Margaret's grandmother had been enslaved, purchased for three dollars and given the last name Charles after her owners. Margaret did not know who her father was,and her mother died when was just 3 weeks old. She and her brother Dennis were raised by their grandmother, only attending school three months of the year in a segregated school system.

There were small black hospitals and community health centers in some of the larger communities, but none in Green County. Most births were at home, incorporating West African traditions, including pepper-based soups to encourage contractions, placing a knife under the bed, and placental ceremonies. Midwives were trained through apprenticeship, learning passed down through generations.

Margaret was 16 when she got pregnant, but she chose not to get married. She hid the pregnancy from her grandmother, until the local midwife spotted her condition and later delivered the baby. Margaret went on to have two more boys, but didn't marry or live with her husband, Randolph Smith, until her grandmother died at the age of 101.

Prior to becoming a midwife, Margaret worked as a cotton farmer, house cleaner, and clothes washer. Due to the sharecropping economic system, her family farm went into debt and she was forced to farm someone else's land. She tells a story of refusing to continue in the back breaking work, risking being lynched for saying no to a white overseer. Instead, she went to work at the post office, saying she would rather be dead than go back to the fields.

It was midwifery that would become Margaret's calling. It provided a chance to use her skills for the women in her community, to help them have control over their births. She delivered a family member's baby while waiting for the doctor to arrive, leading her to train as a traditional midwife. "My grandmother, who was brought to this country and sold, taught me everything I know. She knew these things because she came from Africa. I'm worth millions of dollars for what I've done. I thought I was doing a big thing. I was proud of it. The lives I've saved, going to deliver all these babies."

Although Black women with midwife supported births had lower mortality rates than those delivering with private medical care, they were under increasing regulation. In 1918, Alabama passed a law requiring that midwives take examinations and register with the State Board of Health. A program through Tuskegee trained 3,568 midwives in modern methods and hygiene. Margaret attended this two-week training program along with 300 hundred others, obtained a permit, and registered with a recommendation from a local doctor. Many midwives, including the woman that trained Margaret, Ella Anderson, quit when the permit system was implemented.

In Margaret's first year, she worked part time at the local health department, three rural clinics, and delivering babies in homes. The price for her services were set by the health department, but her patients could not always pay her in cash and would offer her barter instead. Her midwifery career lasted for 28 years. She would provide prenatal care and would stay with women for 2-3 days for the entire length of their birth. There is a documentary, All My Babies, from 1952 that details many of these practices. She deliver edthe children of both black and white families, including the head public health nurse.

In her biography, Margaret discussed challenging births, including a diabetic delivering twins with a postpartum hemorrhage, cords wrapped around the infant's neck, and breech births. She described the need to act quickly in these cases, that the baby must be delivered in 5 minutes or might die. She reported that she only had 5 births that required transport to Tuskegee Hospital, which was three hundred miles away. She never performed an episiotomy. She recalled one story of being left alone with a baby while the mother fled to Florida on a bus.

She also remembered the Civil Rights movement, and her son Houston joining the marches coming in Eutaw: "My oldest son, he knew what was right and what was wrong, because sometimes he spoke down there at the courthouse, and I'd be so scared I didn't know what to do. I begged him to stay home. I didn't want nobody to hurt him. I didn't want to go to the marches, 'cause I didn't want nobody hitting or me or kicking on me or nothing. I saw Martin Luther King...right down here in Eutaw."

By 1969, driven by the voting rights act, Greene County elected African American men to be County Commissioners, Judges and Sheriffs. But Margaret remembers the limits of the progress: "It isn't together like it should be. God made us all. See if we are supposed to unite together...see we know some things and some things, we will never know. The colored folks don't have as much power as the white man, but we have much more than we ever had."

At the same time as the U.S. government was allowing syphilis to run untreated through the community in the Tuskegee Airmen experiments, the medical establishment was working to destroy the practice of African American community midwives. The laws changed quickly when Medicaid and Medicare allowed white doctors to be paid for delivering African American babies. In 1976, Alabama passed laws that brought an end to the tradition of black midwives, and county health departments barred them. This marked the end of the practice for the 150 midwives who were still working. In 1931, there were 3,568 midwives in the state. No lay midwife permits were issued after 1977, and in 2023 there were only 63 licensed Certified Nurse Midwives. The midwives did not have the political power to stop the influence of the white medical establishment.

The Civil Rights era brought the promise of political change, but it did not end the inequalities in healthcare. In the 1940s, 90% of African American babies were born outside of hospitals, a figure that decreased to 46% by 1960. By that same year, the black infant mortality rate was double that of white infants, at 23.2 per 1,000 live births. Greene County opened its first hospital in 1966, but it remained segregated well into the 1980s. Alabama continues to have some of the highest infant mortality rates in the country. In 2018, the black infant mortality rate was still twice that of white infants, with 11.0 deaths per 1,000 live births.

Margaret's life's work as an African American midwife in the South was incredibly important and provides an often-untold story of what has been lost in the push for professionalization and medicalization of birth. In Margaret's 30 years as a midwife, she delivered over 3000 babies. She lived on her farm in Eutaw with her sons Houston and Herman until she passed away in 2004. Margaret was not an activist and her life was confined to a small community. However, as we continue to confront unacceptable racial maternal inequalities, her life and work exemplify the role and importance of the Granny Midwife.

Simone Weil

Simone Weil was a brilliant French-Jewish philosopher who was also a Christian mystic and communist. She spent her short life trying to live her ideals in a deep and profound manner, often putting her at odds with the world. While she had some training as a nurse during World War II, she is included here because of her proposal for front line nurses and her envisioning of the role of nurses as not only caregivers, but as a powerful moral force that could combat the evil of Hitler and Nazism.

Simone was born to a secular Jewish French family in Paris in 1909. Her father was a doctor and her mother was dedicated to raising their children. Both she and her brother were extraordinarily intelligent, and she demonstrated extreme empathy and conviction from a very young age. At age 14, Simone wrote of herself as mediocre, compared to her brilliant brother and hoped that "even though devoid of natural faculties, can penetrate to the kingdom reserved for geniuses if only he longs for truth and perpetually concentrates all his attention upon its attainment."

At 16, Simone enrolled in philosophy studies at the Lycee Henri. She became involved with the communist party, and taught a social education course for working class Parisians. She was awkward and found social interactions challenging. From 1928 to 1931, she studied at the Ecole Normale, an elite teaching academy and earned the nickname "The Red Virgin." She placed first in Philosophy, scoring higher than Simone de Beauvoir, who recalls of their meeting: "She intrigued me because of her great reputation for intelligence and her bizarre outfits. She said in piercing tones that the only one thing mattered these days: the revolution that would feed all the starving people on the earth....I retorted that the problem was not to make men happy, but to help them find a meaning in their existence. She glared at me and said It's clear you've never gone hungry. Our relationship ended right there."

Simone insisted on spending her summers working in physical labor and denied herself physical comforts in solidarity with workers. "Religion makes love manifest, but work...creates respect for the human person and equality; that is why collaboration in work creates enduring friendships for which there is no substitute."

Simone was very active in leftist politics, organizing free philosophy lessons for factory workers, and raising money for unions. She wrote her dissertation on Descartes, a French mathematician and metaphysical philosopher. In 1931, she qualified as a teacher and requested an assignment in a poor industrial community. Instead, she was placed in a quiet small town, Le Puy, where her supervisors felt that she would get into less trouble. For three years she taught philosophy in a series of schools, but caused problems in each of them and was moved regularly. She refused to heat her home, donated almost all her salary, and regularly participated in local political demonstrations. Her mother often traveled to take care of her, finding her housing, and making sure she had enough food.

In 1932, she spent six weeks in Germany and began to write about the conflict between the communists and the Nazis, alarmed by their rising power and use of violence. Simone always had problems with the inconsistencies and hypocrisies of the institutions that she joined. She had incredibly high moral standards and few could meet them. While she had been a long-term supporter of communism, she was very critical of the Soviet government. She also gravitated towards anarchism, and support of unions and direct action.

In 1934, she took a leave of absence from her teaching to work in factories. She was frail and poorly suited for hard labor, and was inevitably fired from these jobs. The work nearly killed her, but she saw her suffering as a way toward redemption and spiritual growth.

After this interruption, she returned to writing and teaching. She wrote the book Oppression and Liberty about individual freedom, political oppression and revolution. Despite her pacifism, she supported the Republicans in the Spanish Civil War, traveling to Barcelona as a member of the press. She did join a military unit, but wasn't allowed in combat or issued a gun, as the leaders were concerned about her competence for fighting. She was only there for a short period when she badly burned herself with hot oil on a campfire and was evacuated back home. She would have been killed if she had stayed, as her entire volunteer unit died shortly after she left.

After a slow recovery from her injuries, Simone traveled to a French Benedictine Abbey. While there, she had a mystical experience that shifted her focus away from politics and toward spirituality. When Hitler invaded Austria, Simone was initially against French intervention, arguing that a German invasion of France might be beneficial if it ended French colonialism, although she later reconsidered this stance.

Living in Paris with her family, Simone made plans to join the resistance and underwent Red Cross nurse training. She also helped refugees who had escaped to Paris, including the exiled Leon Trotsky, a key figure in the Russian Revolution. Trotsky stayed in her family's apartment. Despite their shared opposition to tyranny, he wasn't immune to Simone's sharp criticism, leading to heated arguments during his stay.

In 1941, France surrendered to Hitler's army and Paris was occupied. She resisted leaving the country, although the entire Weil family evacuated to Marseille in Southern France to live under the Vichy government. Simone began to study Roman Catholicism with a blind priest, Father Perrin, engaged in resistance, and wrote a spiritual biography: "I love God, Christ and the Catholic Faith as much as it is possible for so miserably inadequate a creature to love them."

After two years waiting in Marseilles, the Weils were given exit visas to immigrate to the USA via Casablanca. While a refugee in New York, Simone created the idea for a nurse corps and presented it to her friend Maurice Schumann, a leader of the French resistance. She envisioned a corps of ten unarmed nurses deployed to the front lines of war. She emphasized their moral courage rather than professional training, as they would only need basic nursing skills and the ability to comfort the soldiers. These virtuous women, wearing all white uniforms, "should possess in combination a tenderness and cool resolution that enables them to act bravely under enemy fire and the tenderness required for comforting pain and agony.... the triumph of good, in contrast to Hitler's triumph of evil."

Simone hoped that these women would both inspire the Allied forces towards victory and German soldiers towards repentance. "Grace could engender courage, leaving tenderness intact; or it could do the reverse. The mere persistence of a few humane services in the very centre of the battle, the climax of inhumanity, would be a signal defiance of the inhumanity which the enemy has chosen for himself and which he compels us to practice." She was able to get her proposal to French President Charles DeGaul, but he dismissed her idea as insane, and was unsuccessful of getting it to President Roosevelt.

To prepare herself to join the nurses' corps, she took further Red Cross training and obtained a visa to travel to London. She wrote: "The suffering all over the world obsesses me, overwhelms me to the point of annihilating me, and the only way I can release myself from this obsession is to take on a large share of danger and hardship myself."

Although Simone joined the Free French Resistance movement in London, she was not allowed to join the war effort. So she resigned. Increasingly ill and weak, she wrote steadily and finished her final book, *The Need for Roots,* that addresses the essential needs of humans, especially religion over politics, and our obligations to each other to support human flourishing and combat totalitarianism. She wrote about how the essence of goodness is witnessing the suffering of others.

Simone collapsed on April 15th and was hospitalized with tuberculosis. She continued to refuse to eat anything more than the rations of French soldiers while hospitalized, frustrating her medical team. She was baptized by a priest and died of tuberculosis and starvation on August 24, 1942.

Simone was an unusual human, her mysticism and other worldliness like that of Sojourner Truth's, but she had an enormous capacity to imagine a better and more just world. In writing published after she died, *Reflections on the Right Use of School Studies with a View to the Love of God,* she wrote, "The love of our neighbor in all its fullness simply means being able to say to him, What are you going through?" This statement has profound and practical significance to nursing. She understood that empathy is the foundation of ethical engagement between people, and that it is this ability to attend to another that turns love into action. Weil wrote of this attention as a habit where presence and empathy are consciously developed and sustained, providing a vision of nursing as an ethical act, where bearing witness to suffering and offering care becomes a form of love.

Ruth Davidow

Born in Russia in 1911, Ruth Davidow's life spans many of the twentieth centuries most important fights for human rights. Her nursing career spanned the Spanish Civil War to the AIDS epidemic, and she eventually became a documentary filmmaker. While Ruth does not have a full biography written about her, she left behind her films and interviews through the years.

Ruth emigrated with her parents and three siblings to New York at age 3. Her mother worked as a cleaning woman and seamstress, and her father was a shop steward. Her parents were part of Jewish leftist circles in Brooklyn and the Lower East Side. Her mother was a member of the International Ladies Garment Workers Union, taking her daughter to rallies and selling the communist newspaper *The Daily Worker*.

Ruth had thought about becoming a lawyer. But she chose nursing instead. Her decision was influenced by her father's diagnosis of tuberculosis: "I decided I must simply become a nurse. I would be independent for the rest of my life...the work of a nurse was always essential. I could support my mother."

In 1936, she attended nursing school at Brooklyn Jewish Hospital. Like other programs of the time, training was 7 days a week with only one half a day off. "After the first year, another student and I were responsible for 56 patients. I was trained in pharmacology, surgery, midwifery...But I also began to engage in politics. It was during the Great Depression. My training as a nurse began to form my views on this. When you visit a patient at home, you don't take care of only him or her, you teach health care to the family."

Like many leftists, she was drawn to the fight in the Spanish Civil War. In 1931, King Alfonso of Spain abdicated the throne. The newly elected socialist Spanish Republic pushed for land and education reform and separation of church and state. The military, Catholic church, and the aristocracy joined together to fight these progressive reforms. Thirty-five hundred Americans created a coalition of anarchist, anti-fascist, communist, and socialist as a popular front against Francisco Franco and the military. Who were supported by Hitler and Mussolini. Despite popular support and Ernest Hemingway's war reporting, the U.S. would not aid the popular front. Twenty-seven European countries and the U.S. signed a non-intervention pact, which ensured that Franco and the fascist party would win the war.

Ruth was moved by the cause, realizing that Hitler and Mussolini wanted to take over the whole world. She joined the Lincoln Brigade and traveled to Spain to provide nursing care to the resistance. The U.S. State Department prohibited travel to Spain, threatening to revoke citizenship for any participants. Nine hundred brigade members entered Spain by pretending to be tourists. Ruth remembered: "The Lincoln Brigade were kids, and were unprepared....we would work for hours, filthy. Shortage of equipment, sharpening our needles on stones, as long as there is a struggle for justice, there will be battles."

As Hitler invaded Austria, Franco and the military devastated the resistance. All International Brigades were withdrawn, holding a parade in Barcelona as they left, Ruth continued to raise money before the Republic fell in 1939. She returned to the United States and married Fred Keller, a Union and Lincoln Brigade Organizer.

Later, Ruth would tell the stories of the Lincoln Brigade through her documentary films, *The Good Fight, Their Cause Was Liberty* and Academy Award nominee *Forever Activists.*Spain made her an honorary citizen in recognition of her service. Ruth continued both her activism and nursing for her entire life, across many different causes.

Ruth moved to San Francisco in 1955 and received a degree in public health from the University of California at San Francisco, working as a public health nurse. From 1960 to 1962, she worked in Havana in post-revolution Cuba. In 1965, she traveled to Mississippi as a Freedom Rider for the Medical Committee for Human Rights, which organized health care to support the Civil Rights movement.

As a filmmaker, she produced 21 films on such subjects as health, geriatrics and political movements, including *Do No Harm, Love Letter to Cuba'* and *My Brother Michael,* (a profile of her brother who had been a reporter for the *Daily Worker* and lived in Moscow for many years). She provided health care to Native American protestors in The Occupation of Alcatraz, a 19-month long protest organized and led by eighty Native Americans, to reclaim the land from the federal government. This protest sparked Native American activism and tribal self-rule and was one of the most important Native American Movements in the twentieth century.

She founded a health clinic in Haight Ashbury to provide health care to people who used drugs in the 1980s. This placed her at the center of the start of the AIDS epidemic, when health care professionals in San Francisco and New York were just starting to be aware of the disease among homosexual men. At the time, they didn't know how it was spread, how to treat it, or how it attacked the human immune system. Only a few brave healthcare providers would treat them. Ruth also traveled to the Third International Women's Conference in Beijing in her eighties.

Although she was not famous or influential, she provided a template for how to utilize nursing skills to support activism and to make the struggle for justice a lifelong one. She died in San Francisco in 1999. While she did not leave much writing behind, many of her films can still be viewed on YouTube.

Salaria Kea O'Reilly

Salaria Kea was an African American nurse and activist who was also drawn into the fight for freedom during the Spanish Civil War. Born in 1913, in Jim Crow Georgia, she moved with her mom and three siblings to Ohio when her father was killed working at a psychiatric hospital. For unknown reasons, her mother returned to Georgia, leaving Salaria and her siblings to be brought up by the Jackson family, along with their own five children.

While growing up, Salaria worked in the office of a local African American physician, who convinced her to attend nursing school. Because of racial segregation in nursing education, she moved to attend the Harlem Hospital Training School. She joined others protesting segregated dining by turning over a table in the cafeteria. This protest led them to successfully integrate the dining rooms at the hospital.

Salaria graduated in 1934, first working in a TB ward and then at the OB department of the Harlem Hospital. She was outspoken about the unacceptable conditions, including one nurse trying to care for fifty babies and an outbreak of diarrhea killing three to five babies a day. She helped organize the Harlem community to publicly protest the conditions and demanded the ward be closed until an investigation was completed.

Salaria was very politically active outside of the hospital as well, attending lectures and discussions about local, national, and international events. When Mussolini invaded Ethiopia, she and other health care professionals raised enough funds to supply a 75-bed hospital for the Ethiopian troops.

Salaria then turned her activism towards the Spanish Revolution. Five years after the Spanish Republic was democratically elected, General Franco led a fascist military coup, backed by the Nazis against the leftist government of Spain.

The Republic asked for support from the U.S. and Great Britain, who instead imposed an embargo that made it impossible for them to obtain firearms or medical supplies. 35,000 volunteers, many who were communists, from 53 countries formed International Brigades to come to the aid of the Spanish Republic. Soldiers came from all over the world to help the Spanish Republic; Czech, Cubans, Mexicans, Japanese, French, Ethiopians, and Americans all united to help defeat fascism in Spain.

Salaria first attempted to volunteer with the American Red Cross but was denied because of her race. In 1937, she sailed to Spain with twelve nurses and physicians (she was the only African American female) as part of the American Medical Unit, or Lincoln Brigade. The experience was profound, "I went to Spain to do what we are all here to do, to help people. I had no problem with being black. It was like being with a family."

Upon arrival, the Lincoln Brigade worked together to open a field hospital near Madrid. The conditions were difficult, as they were short of supplies and food and living with Spanish peasants. Soon the hospital was filled with injured soldiers from the front. They not only treated soldiers but tried to provide medical care for Spanish peasants. The work was brutal and difficult, but Salaria saw it as part of a larger purpose and a global struggle for freedom and equality. She saw that the fate of African Americans was tied to the global freedom of others. She felt she was fighting for larger causes than just Spain. Salaria noted that she was valued and able to work free from racial prejudice or false restrictions for the first time in her life.

In early April 1933, the brigade moved from Madrid to set up field hospitals at the front. They were quickly overwhelmed and had to evacuate. Salaria describes: "That evening about seven o'clock patients began to pour in by hundreds. All that night we worked to treat as many as possible and start them on the way further behind the front lines. When morning came, we had nineteen patients left. These were wounded so badly that it did not seem safe to move them. By eight o'clock that morning we were visited by five fascist planes..... They turned their machine guns on us and began firing – terrifically, continuously."

During this time, Salaria was separated from her unit and hitchhiked to Barcelona to rejoin the American forces at their hospital. Barcelona was being continuously bombed, with deliberate targeting of civilians, children, and humanitarian workers. She appeared in two movies *Heart of Spain*, and *Return to Life*.

In March 1938, Salaria was badly injured when a bomb exploded near her and left her partially buried. She was sent home and turned her energy to organize medical supplies. She also worked to publicize the struggle. She was featured in a pamphlet *A Negro Nurse in Republican Spain* and went on a speaking and publicity tour.

Salaria married John Joseph O'Reilly, an Irish ambulance driver she met in Spain. They had to face constant racism over their integrated marriage. In the beginning of 1944, Salaria started working as a volunteer nurse for the U.S. Army Nurses Corps as part of their first group of African American nurses. She also worked in several hospitals, coordinating staff desegregation, before she died in 1990.

Albertina Sisulu

Albertina Sisulu, was born Nontsikelelo Mnyilas in the Tsomo District of Transkei in South Africa. She was one of eight children born to Bonilizwe and Monikazi Thethiwe, members of the Khosa nation. Albertina attended a Catholic mission school until she was 11, when her father died of mining related lung disease. She had to leave school to take care of her younger siblings.

In 1936, she won a scholarship to attend Mariazell College, a boarding school a hundred miles from home. Two years later, she returned home and was expected to enter an arranged marriage. She did not want to marry. She planned to become a nun until a priest encouraged her to study nursing so she could support her family.

In 1939, she was accepted as a trainee nurse at Johannesburg Non-European Hospital. According to her daughter-in-law, Elinor, who wrote her biography, Albertina "took to nursing like a duck to water. Her upbringing inculcated high standards of cleanliness, discipline, and a strong work ethic stood her in good stead. Her compassionate and empathetic nature made it easy for her to relate to patients. She enjoyed the lectures and the clinical work. She took great pride in her starched white uniform."

Johannesburg was racially segregated. The racism of the medical system was illustrated by a mass casualty event where white staff refused to treat injured black Africans. The history of apartheid in South Africa goes back to the 17th century, when the Dutch East India company and the British established colonies, fighting each other over control of the land. During the Boer War, the British defeated the Dutch, and started to build an apartheid government where black Africans could not vote or own property.

In 1941, Albertina's mother died. She began dating Walter Sisulu, who founded the African National Congress with Nelson Mandela. They married three years later. and she converted from Catholicism to Walter's Anglican religion. Albertina took a position as a midwife at Johannesburg General Hospital. Albertina and Walter were equally dedicated to their family and South Africa's freedom. In their first year of marriage ,Albertina worked as a nurse, gave birth to a son, Max, and was engaged in political activism.

It was a turbulent year in South Africa with a miner's strike, protests for civil rights, and calls for land reform. In 1947, Walter became first Secretary General of the African National Congress. The white National Party won elections by promising to further restrict black's rights. The Sisulu home was a center for activism for the entire community and became a focus of government oppression.

Albertina was a member of the ANC Women's League, but political action was limited because the ANC only allowed one parent to put themselves at risk of jail at a time. While Albertina was visiting her hometown with their children, Walter was arrested for the first time for not carrying a pass. In between his arrests, Walter traveled to London, Israel, and the Soviet Union to build support for their struggle for freedom.

In September 1955, the government held a mass raid with Walter being among the five hundred arrested. In response the ANC women organized a 20,000-woman protest. Albertina went to jail for three weeks with Mandela serving as her lawyer. In 1958, Walter underwent a trial for treason and faced long term imprisonment. This same year the South African Nursing Council enforced discrimination by demanding all nurses and students carry identity passes. Albertina and the ANC Women's League organized a mass demonstration of a thousand women and the Nursing Council dropped the demand. Albertina was imprisoned for organizing the protest and used her nursing skills to take care of Nelson's second wife Winnie during a difficult pregnancy.

The 1960s were the height of apartheid and the Sisulu's resistance was very dangerous. On March 21, 1960, an anti-pass protest ended in the Sharpeville massacre, with 69 peaceful protesters killed and 2000 activists arrested. Walter and Nelson Mandela were frequently on trial, in jail, or in hiding. Albertina's children remember almost daily police raids during this time. In the early 1960s, the government enacted new laws, including the death penalty for sabotage and the authority to hold suspects for 90 days without charges.

Albertina was arrested under these new laws in an attempt to force Walter out of hiding, as there was a risk of their children being taken into state custody. Their son, Max, went into exile in Tanzania and later to the Soviet Union. When Walter was again arrested and put on trial, Albertina took on the responsibility of financially supporting her family. She sent four of her children to boarding school in Swaziland for their safety, partially with money raised by Anglican priests. They had to sneak out of the country since they did not have their own passports.

She also helped support the families of other prisoners. Walter and Nelson's trial ended with guilty verdicts and they were sentenced to life in prison at Robben Island where the conditions were horrible. Albertina was put on restriction, unable to leave Johannesburg or meet with others. She was only able to visit Walter after months of planning. Money was extremely tight, and she was under a great deal of stress. Albertina would meet with other activists by having them visit her at her clinic pretending to be patients. Her daughter in law remembered,:"She never seemed to rest." In 1969, her house arrest was extended for another 5 years, and she had to be very careful to avoid re-arrest. Albertina was still on restriction and had to check in with the police every week and couldn't leave her township.

In the 1970's, the anti-apartheid movement became more radical. The government oppression intensified the debate within the ANC about the use of violence. The government moved to enforce speaking of Afrikaans in Soweto schools, even though neither teachers nor students spoke the language. Students, including the Sisulu children, started protesting and 600 students were killed. Albertina recalled: "One day the nurses called me, saying that they saw Jongi and Nkuli running past the clinic. I didn't know what to do because the police were shooting. And I just thought even if they are killed, I must see their corpses. Because in most cases people didn't know what had happened to their children. We believed they were being dumped at night by helicopters in the swamps of Moflo, and that the area was smelling because of the bodies of the children that were there."

Her children survived but they were arrested, beaten and detained for weeks. Albertina helped protestors and those in danger leave the country, despite being repeatedly arrested. She spent two years in prison, seven months of which was in solitary confinement. Her son, Zwelakhe, the leader of Black Media Workers Association was arrested under terrorism charges.

By 1980, ANC began to take more direct action to free Mandela and his fellow prisoners. The student protests and escalation of violence started to gain international attention. Albertina was elected co-president of the United Democratic Front, organizing different interest groups against apartheid. From her speech in honor of the UDF: "Sons and daughters of Africa, to me today I'm a great big mother, for today our multiracial baby is born, for today our baby that will rule this South Africa in future is born, the multiracial baby, the United Democratic Front, Which is uniting the people to speak with one voice, which is uniting the people to tell the truth, which is uniting the people to say no to the Koornhof laws, which is uniting the people to say away with the new constitution. Because it doesn't give us freedom mothers was in jail. I knew I had a new baby in the crib although I was in jail. I was very happy to have this baby, but unfortunately for me, it was taken away from me before I could see it. But I'm happy to say today, all those people have come to witness that the baby ...is march the people to freedom."

While Albertina was out on bail, she took a nursing job with Dr. Abu Baker Asvat, an ethnically Indian doctor and co-founder of AZAPO political party, who ran a clinic in Soweto in addition to his outreach and health activism for people throughout South Africa. He made it possible for her to be employed while she was under restriction, and to accommodate her organizing work and visiting Walter in prison. Even in her sixties, her daughter-in-law, remembers :"She would work a full day in the clinic, then spend 3-4 hours on meetings, and weekends were filled with meetings, women organizers and interviews with journalists. She was calm and unflappable and did not tolerate whining."

In early 1989, Dr. Asvat, her boss and close friend, was shot in his clinic, dying in Albertina's arms. While two men were charged with the murder, it was widely believed that Winnie Mandela was responsible to keep him from testifying about crimes he had witnessed. This tragedy occurred as the political situation started to change. Albertina traveled to Sweden, France, the U.K., and the U.S.

for her anti-violence activism, encouraging George Bush and Margaret Thatcher to help end apartheid.

When F. W. DeKlerk was elected as president, Albertina's ban was lifted and Walter and her other children were released from prison. A few months later, De Klerk legalized the African National Congress and released Nelson Mandela. The Sisulus didn't pause in their fight for equality as the ANC became the dominant political organization in South Africa, representing thirty million blacks speaking eleven languages.

Walter and Albertina traveled to Singapore, Australia, Soviet Union, and North America to share the story of their struggle. In April 1994, Mandela was democratically elected president of South Africa. Albertina, Lindi, and Max Sisulu were elected to parliament. Another son, Zwelakhe, was the first black person to head the South African Broadcasting Corporation.

Albertina left parliament in 1999. She died in 2011, eight years after her husband of fifty years. She was survived by 5 children, 26 grandchildren and an entire country who remembers her as "Ma Sisulu" and "Mother of the Nation" Nelson Mandela wrote in his autobiography:"There can be no greater and inspiring example in the history of our organization, and our country. A couple who every deed speaks of leadership that made the kind of difference that brought us to where we are today as a country and people. The unstinting commitment to the common good and to the service of the people filled their life."

Marie Branch

Marie Branch was a nurse, academic, and Black Panther who was active through the late 1960s and 1970s. There is no biography of her life, but she did leave behind her writing and a record of her political work. She was also an early academic supporter of anti-racist philosophy and practice in nursing education.

The Black Panthers were founded in 1966 by Bobby Seale and Hughie Newton. It was organized to protect African Americans from the state and offer a range of community services. They were inspired by revolutionaries Mao Zedong, Che Guevara, (an Argentinian Doctor), and Frantz Fanon, (a Caribbean psychiatrist). Guevara wrote: "The doctor, the medical worker, must go to the core of the new work, to treat what has been the inheritance of centuries of repression and total submission."

In Oakland, the Black Panthers started their community service initiatives, including health care as one of their ten item platforms: "We believe that the government must provide, free of charge, for the people, health facilities which will not only treat our illnesses, but will also develop preventive medical programs to guarantee our future survival." In April 1970, Bobby Seale issued a directive for all party chapters to open People's Free Medical Clinics. These clinics were meant to be African American run institutions that offered a different model of healthcare, focused on the knowledge of lay people rather than the professional medical- industrial complex, and staffed by patient advocates. Eventually clinics opened in thirteen cities across the U.S., operating independently and responsible for their own funding.

Marie was an Assistant Professor of Nursing at the University of California, Los Angeles when she co-founded the Bunchy Carter Black Panther Party's Free Clinic in Los Angeles in 1969. Marie recounted that most of the clinics were run by volunteer African American women, and that she was the only African American health care professional at the L.A. Clinic. The clinic relied on volunteers to provide gynecology, screenings, and childhood immunizations. Volunteers were held accountable to the community and their patients and would be let go if they didn't provide respectful care.

The Panthers also engaged in medical activism, challenging the creation of the UCLA Center for the Study and Reduction of Violence, an initiative that sought to investigate the biological basis of race and violence. The Center planned to conduct psychiatric studies on people of color and other vulnerable populations. The Panthers defeated the creation of the center by organizing with unions, feminist and student rights organizations against the biologization of violence.

In March 1972, Marie and eighteen other Panthers, including Angela Davis and physician Tolbert Small, traveled to China. They wanted to explore China's de-professionalization of medicine through their barefoot doctors program. They were inspired to fight against the expertise model of medicine and to "overturn the idea of bourgeois medicine to fight medical discrimination." Branch wrote about her experiences in *A Black American Nurse Visits the People's Republic of China*.

While in China, she observed that health education was widely available and more egalitarian than in the U.S. She learned about acupuncture and witnessed nursing students who started out as hospital housekeepers before they studied nursing. They observed

China's healthcare models, including mobile clinics in rural areas and China's barefoot doctors program where people were trained in their own villages. The health care workers in China combined traditional medicine with Western medical practices, in contrast to the U.S. where traditional practices are generally ignored. She was inspired by this work and saw the clear benefits these innovations could provide for people in the United States. Her commitment to improving healthcare and nursing education extended into her role as nursing professor at UCLA.

In 1976, she wrote *Models for Providing Cultural Diversity in Nursing Curricula,* emphasizing the importance of ethnic and cultural diversity in nursing education. She continued her work through 1985, authoring articles on *Self-Care for Black Perspectives* and co editing *Providing Safe Nursing Care for Ethnic People of Color.* She wrote that nurse educators "need to find the way to light a fire in our students, to instill in them a desire and a compulsion to become instrumental in bringing their skills to people in need. Is it not essential that nursing students are provided with experiences that will prepare them for work with diverse cultural groups in poverty level communities by expanding their value systems to include an appreciation of lifestyles other than their own?" She called for nursing education to focus on:

1. High risk population groups in impoverished urban and rural areas

2. Mental health related problems, including addiction

3. Public health education

4. Community social issues related to those conditions that interfere with health and well-being.

Marie championed the need for clinical immersion, so that nurses from one background could better understand people different from themselves. She also called for nurses' accountability to ethnic minorities in the quality of their care. Marie was the project director for one of the earliest efforts to address cultural diversity in nursing curriculum. She led a project to create models for cultural diversity in nursing curricula from nursing schools in the western U.S. The goals of this project included hiring faculty and staff from various ethnic groups, recruiting ethnic students of colors, orientation and education programs, faculty development, and inclusion of culturally relevant information and experiences throughout the curriculum.

Marie worked on an affirmative action task force of the American Nurses Association, writing a section called *Toward Quality Nursing Care for a Multiracial Society.* She wrote: "Quality care is not possible under the circumstances of today's health care system, and the quality care depends upon effective affirmative action programs which addresses underrepresentation and underutilization in nursing, referencing the 1964 Federal Civil Right legislation, and 1972 guidelines for affirmative action in education, including nurses, Quality care requires recognition of differing perspectives in planning, giving, and evaluating care for all. The standards for care currently in effect are suitable for the people which they were designed for: Caucasian, primarily middle class."

Branch eventually left the nursing profession, becoming a chiropractor in Los Angeles. Her dedication and advocacy work allows those to continue to follow in her footsteps and provide a pathway to a more equitable nursing profession.

Shirley Willer

Shirley Willer is the last of the stories in this book and provides the most modern example of nurse activism. An early gay rights activist in the U.S. She used her work as a nurse to support herself before leaving to dedicate herself full time to her activism. Most of what we know about Shirley's life was from a series of interviews she did with Eric Marcus, who compiled an oral history of the American gay rights movement.

Shirley was born on September 26, 1922, in Chicago. When she was 8, her mother Teresa left to raise her and her sister away from their father, an abusive alcoholic. Shirley was academically successful and went on to get an undergraduate degree at the University of Chicago and then a master's at the University of Iowa.

She first realized she was a lesbian during a nursing lecture at age 19. Her professor was discussing the existence of women attracted to other women and not men. Willer stated that at this moment, she thought to herself: "Oh, gee, I'm one of those things!" She hadn't realized she was different from others and didn't understand other women's attraction to men. Willer then talked with her professor about her feelings and was sent to a psychiatrist for treatment. She knew that there was nothing wrong with her and that she was free to love whomever she wanted.

Willer came out to her mother soon after. While her mother was initially upset, shequickly expressed her support. She gave Shirley the book The Well of Loneliness by Radclyffe Hall, a 1920s lesbian novel. She had a more challenging experience after coming out to society in general, realizing she was considered by many to be 'a pervert'.

After completing her nursing training, Willer started working as a Registered Nurse at a hospital in Chicago. She had to work 16-hour shifts because of WWII staffing shortages. Her nursing career ranged from psychiatric nursing to working at the Argonne National Library, where the atomic bomb was completed. She was upfront with being queer at all her jobs and said it generally was not a problem, although she was fired once because a co-worker complained about her.

Shirley connected with the underground gay community, and was radicalized after she was arrested in Chicago because she was out at 11:00 pm wearing pants, looking for a lesbian bar. Her arrest and being called a queer as a slander made her angry. She discusses attending gay balls where women could dress in tuxedos and the men could wear dresses. These events were run by the mafia and exposed the participants to extortion and violence.

Shirley remembers her first gay friends were other nurses, effeminate gay veterans she met after they returned from WWII. She discussed one of these friends, a man named Barney, who was working as a nurse during the night shift while attending medical school during the day. He was badly burnt in a house fire and received terrible care because of homophobia, dying in a Catholic Hospital at age 24. "Barney's death probably had a great deal to do with why I've spent a large part of my life being angry. And it wasn't just me. We were angry people."

Around this time, she met and began organizing with attorney Pearl Hart. Their activism was torn between the need to keep a low profile for safety or to be more open about their gay identity.

Shirley started a group to help teenagers who had been thrown out of their homes, helping them with housing and funding for attending school. Their early activism efforts were not openly political but involved creating networks and supporting others. "We knew at the time that we couldn't do much to change laws in Chicago, but we could give these kids a sense of self-esteem. We could show them that what we did, they could do. We could have a life, a good life, a comfortable life, earn a good living, own cars, and be citizens with all the duties, responsibilities and benefits." She continued to live this example in San Francisco with a nursing job and supportive family. Her activism focused on direct mutual aid, offering an open door for homeless gay youth, and adopting a transgendered child who died young.

In 1962, Shirley moved to New York City, where she joined the Daughters of Bilitis (DOB), the first lesbian rights organization in the U.S., founded in San Francisco in 1955. During her first DOB event, she met founding member Marion Glass, who became her life partner.

Shirley left nursing to work as a gay civil rights activist through the DOB, becoming the national president of the organization in 1966. This work was funded by a wealthy and anonymous donor with a goal to build DOB chapters nationally, and publishing *The Ladder*, a national lesbian magazine. "I traveled all over the country through the mid -1960s, helping to form DOB chapters and organizations. In whatever town I was going, I got hold of people I knew and said that they were coming there to help form an organization, and then they would do as they pleased. I was lucky in that I found a sponsor who helped me with my travel money. This very prominent woman was gay, but there was no way she could do the work I was doing. She's from one of the first ten families, and I could do this without getting into any trouble. She also financed the printing of *The Ladder* and funded legal work in New York & San Francisco. No one will ever give credit for this woman, but she has the satisfaction of going down the street and seeing a couple of guys or a couple of girls walking hand in hand, of seeing the Mafia lose control of the gay bars."

DOB was part of the "homophile" movement that worked to remove stigma from being gay and led the way to later gay rights movements. Shirley was very clear about being confident with her lesbian identity; she felt no shame or embarrassment and wanted the same for others. Because of her work, the *New York Times* stopped using the word pervert to describe gays. She and Marion also taught classes to psychiatrists about their lived experience as lesbians and to stop diagnosing homosexuality as a mental illness.

Shirley's activism ended in disappointment. The Daughters of Bilitis were too cautious for Shirley. She quit the organization in 1968 as it began to fall apart. As she told Eric Marcus, "I felt that I had really failed. I saw no future for DOB. For me this was like my religion. To have it explode in your face was not a successful ending to a career."

Shirley and Marion spent the last years of their lives in Key West, Florida, where they opened and ran a rock shop and became involved with the growing lesbian and gay community there. Shirley passed away on New Year's Eve in 1999, witnessing the remarkable growth and impact of her work as well as the significant strides made by the gay rights movement in the United States. Her contributions played a crucial role in advocating for LGBTQ+ rights. She lived to see many of the successes that continue to shape the movement today.

References

Hildegard von Bingen

Flanagan, S. (1989). Hildegard of Bingen: A Visionary Life. London, UK: Routledge. Lerman, K. (1995, May 24). The life and works of Hildegard von Bingen (1098-1179).

Internet History Sourcebooks Project, Fordham University. Retrieved from https://sourcebooks.fordham.edu/med/hildegarde.asp

Hildegard von Bingen. (1999). Physica: The Complete English Translation of Her Classic Work on Health and Healing. Rochester, VT: Healing Arts Press.

Maddocks, F. (2013). Hildegard von Bingen: The Woman of Her Age. London, UK: Faber & Faber.

Sor Juana Inés de la Cruz

Paz, O. (1988). Sor Juana, Or the Traps of Faith. Cambridge, MA: Harvard University Press.

Sor Juana Inés de la Cruz. (1994). The Writings of Sor Juana Inés de la Cruz. New York, NY: Penguin Classics. Project Vox. (n.d.).

Sor Juana Inés de la Cruz (1648-1695). Retrieved from https://projectvox.org/sor-juana-1648-1695/

Sojourner Truth

The Sojourner Truth Project. (n.d.). Retrieved from https://www.thesojournertruthproject.com Biography.com Editors. (n.d.). Sojourner Truth. Biography. Retrieved from https://www.biography.com/activists/sojourner-truth

National Park Service. (n.d.). Sojourner Truth. Retrieved from https://www.nps.gov/articles/sojourner-truth.htm

Truth, S., & Gilbert, O. (1850). Narrative of Sojourner Truth: A Northern Slave, Emancipated from Bodily Servitude by the State of New York, in 1828. Boston, MA: J. B. Yerrinton and Son.

Painter, N. I. (1996). Sojourner Truth: A Life, A Symbol. New York, NY: W. W. Norton & Company.

Ontario Nurses' Association. (n.d.). Hidden figures: Celebrating 100 years of Black women in nursing. Retrieved from https://www.ona.org/wp-content/uploads/hidden-figures.pdf

Documenting the American South. (n.d.). Sojourner Truth. University of North Carolina at Chapel Hill. Retrieved from https://docsouth.unc.edu/highlights/sojournertruth.html

Stowe, H. B. (1863, April). Sojourner Truth, the Libyan Sibyl. The Atlantic Monthly. Retrieved from https://www.theatlantic.com/magazine/archive/1863/04/sojourner-truth-the-libyan-sibyl/308775/

National Park Service. (n.d.). Sojourner Truth: Ain't I A Woman? Retrieved from https://www.nps.gov/articles/sojourner-truth.htm

Mary Seacole

Robinson, J. (2004). Mary Seacole. New York, NY: Carroll & Graf.

Messmer, P. R., & Parchment, Y. (1998). Mary Grant Seacole: The first nurse practitioner. Clinical Excellence for Nurse Practitioners: The International Journal of NPACE, 2(1), 47-51.

Rappaport, H. (2005). In Search of Mary Seacole. New York, NY: Vintage. Seacole, M. (1857). Wonderful Adventures of Mrs. Seacole in Many Lands. London, UK: James Blackwood.

The Victorian Web. (2002, April 30). Another Florence Nightingale? The rediscovery of Mary Seacole. National University of Singapore. https://victorianweb.org/history/crimea/seacole.html

Pouchet, S. (n.d.). The enigma of arrival: The wonderful adventures of Mrs. Seacole in many lands. African American Review. Retrieved from https://www.proquest.com/docview/209808159?sourcetype=Scholarly%20Journals

Margaret Fuller

Deiss, J. J. (1969). The Roman Years of Margaret Fuller. New York, NY: Thomas Y. Crowell Company.

Matteson, J. (2012). The Lives of Margaret Fuller: A Biography. New York, NY: W. W. Norton & Company.

Baker, C. (1997). Emerson among the Eccentrics: A Group Portrait. New York, NY: Viking.

Fuller, M. (1978). American Feminism: Key Source Documents, 1848-1920. New York, NY: Oxford University Press.

Fuller, M. (1992). The Essential Margaret Fuller. Rutgers University Press. Rostenberg, L. (1940). Margaret fuller's Roman diary. The Journal of Modern History, 12(2), 209-220.

Bridget "Biddy" Mason

Hickman, K. (2023). Brave hearted. Bloomsbury Publishing.

Kinney Williams, J. (2001). Bridget "Biddy" Mason: From slave to businesswoman. Morgan Reynolds. Retrieved from https://archive.org/details/bridgetbiddymaso00will

Smith, E. (1997). Epic lives: One hundred black women who made a difference. Visible Ink Press. Retrieved from https://archive.org/details/epiclivesonehund00smit

Taylor, Q. (1998). In search of the racial frontier: African Americans in the American West, 1528–1990. W.W. Norton & Company.

Hayden, D. (1989). Biddy Mason's Los Angeles, 1856–1891. California History, 68(3), 86–99. https://doi.org/10.2307/25158491

Livingston, M. (2018, August 18). Honoring the legacy and 200th birthday of slave-turned-entrepreneur Biddy Mason. Los Angeles Times. Retrieved from https://www.latimes.com/local/lanow/la-me-biddy-mason-memorial-story-20180818-story.html

National Park Service. (n.d.). Biddy Mason. Retrieved from https://www.nps.gov/people/biddymason.htm

African American Registry. (n.d.). Slavery to entrepreneur: Biddy Mason. Retrieved from https://web.archive.org/web/20140506090944/http://www.aaregistry.org/historic_events/view/slavery-entrepreneur-biddy-mason

Black Voice News. (n.d.). Bridget "Biddy" Smith Mason: Her legacy among the Mormons. Retrieved from https://web.archive.org/web/20140808042500/http://www.blackvoicenews.com/inside-pages/religion/39294-bridget-biddy-smith-mason-her-legacy-among-the-mormons.html

Walt Whitman

Reynolds, D. S. (1995). Walt Whitman's America: A Cultural Biography. New York, NY: Alfred A. Knopf.

Whitman Archive. (n.d.). Encyclopedia entry. Retrieved from https://whitmanarchive.org/item/encyclopedia_entry8 Barbian L, Sledzik PS, Reznick JS. Remains of War: Walt Whitman, Civil War Soldiers, and the Legacy of Medical Collections. Mus Hist J. 2012 Jan;5(1):7-28. doi: 10.1179/mhj.2012.5.1.7. PMID: 22741042; PMCID: PMC3381362.

Hsu, D. (2010). Walt Whitman: An American Civil War nurse who witnessed the advent of modern American medicine. Archives of environmental & occupational health, 65(4), 238-239.

Strandberg, V. H. (n.d.). Biography. DukeSpace. Retrieved from https://dukespace.lib.duke.edu/server/api/core/bitstreams/74eef99c-2cdf-4226-b642-fc3671624db3/content

Harriet Tubman

Dunbar, E. A. (2019). She Came to Slay: The Life and Times of Harriet Tubman. New York, NY: 37 Ink.

Foner, E. (2015). Gateway to Freedom: The Hidden History of the Underground Railroad. New York, NY: W.W. Norton & Company.

Bradford, S. H. (1869). Harriet, the Moses of Her People. New York, NY: Geo. R. Lockwood & Son.

Larson, K. C. (2004). Bound for the Promised Land: Harriet Tubman, Portrait of an American Hero. New York, NY: Ballantine Books. Harriet Tubman. Retrieved from http://www.harriet-tubman.org

Kusomote Ine

Harding, J. (2020). The Japanese: A history in twenty lives. Penguin Random House UK.

Yoshimura, A. (2016). Siebold's Daughter: A Novel (R. Rubinger, Trans.). MerwinAsia

Nakamura, F. (2008). Working the Siebold network: Kusumoto Ine and Western learning in nineteenth-century Japan. Japanese Studies Bulletin of the Japanese Studies Association of Australia, 28(2), 153-171. https://doi.org/10.1080/10371390802249172

Rubinger, R. (2013). The Search for Siebold's Daughter: Fact and Fiction in the Work of Yoshimura Akira. Japanese Studies, 33(2), 135–146. https://doi.org/10.1080/10371397.2013.816241

Choperena, A and Fairman, J. Kusumoto Ine: A Remarkable Woman in Meiji Restoration Japan. Not Even Past. Retrieved from https://noteevenpast.org/kusumoto-ine-a-remarkable- woman-in-meiji-restoration-japan/

Louisa May Alcott

Alcott, L. M. (1868). Little women; or, Meg, Jo, Beth, and Amy. Roberts Brothers.

Thomas, Peyton. (2022, December 24). Did the mother of young adult literature identify as a man? The New York Times. Retrieved from https://www.nytimes.com/2022/12/24/opinion/did- the-mother-of-young-adult-literature-identify-as-a-man.html

Seiple, S. (2019). Louisa on the front lines: Louisa May Alcott in the Civil War. New York, NY: Seal Press.

Choperena, A., & Fairman, J. (2017). Louisa May Alcott and Hospital Sketches: An innovative approach to gender and nursing professionalization. Journal of Advanced Nursing, 73(12), 3057-3065. https://doi.org/10.1111/jan.13510

Alcott, L. M. (1863). Hospital sketches. Boston: James Redpath.

Williams, R. (2016, February 26). Louisa May Alcott - Civil War Nurse. National Museum of Civil War Medicine. Retrieved from https://www.civilwarmed.org/alcott/

Sullivan, Caroline. (2022). Alcott's secret identity. Retrieved from https://sites.duke.edu/unsuitable/alcotts-secret-identity/

VCU School of Nursing. (n.d.). Flashback: Louisa May Alcott. Retrieved from https://nursing.virginia.edu/news/flashback-alcott/

Lavinia Dock

Dock, L. L. (n.d.). Lavinia Dock: A biography. Retrieved From https://onlinebooks.library.upenn.edu/webbin/book/lookupname?key=Dock%2C%20Lavinia%20L%2E%2C%201858%2D1956

Dock, L. L. (1890). Text-book of materia medica for nurses. New York: G.P. Putnam's Sons. Harvard Library. (n.d.). Lavinia Dock: A biography [Digital image]. Retrieved from https://iiif.lib.harvard.edu/manifests/view/drs:457646150$225i Philips, Deborah (1999). "Healthy Heroines: Sue Barton, Lillian Wald, Lavinia Lloyd Dock and the Henry Street Settlement": Journal of American Studies, 33(1), 65–82. https://doi.org/10.1017/S0021875898006070

Garofalo, M. E., & Fee, E. (2015). Lavinia Dock (1858–1956): Picketing, parading, and protesting. American Journal of Public Health, 105(2), 276– 277. https://doi.org/10.2105/AJPH.2014.302021

Roberts, M. M. (1956). Lavinia Lloyd Dock—Nurse, Feminist, Internationalist. AJN The American Journal of Nursing, 56(2), 176-179.

https://journals.lww.com/ajnonline/abstract/1956/02000/lavinia_lloyd_dock_nurse,_feminist,.14.aspx

Smith, S. M. (2002). Nursing as social responsibility: Implications for democracy from the life perspective of Lavinia Lloyd Dock (1858–1956). Louisiana State University and Agricultural & Mechanical College. https://repository.lsu.edu/cgi/viewcontent.cgi?article=1104&context=gradschool_dissertations

Lillian Wald

Henry Street Settlement. (n.d.). Retrieved from https://www.henrystreet.org Social Welfare History Project. (2017, February 4). Lillian D. Wald (1867–1940) – Nurse, Social Worker, Women's Rights Activist and Founder of Henry Street Settlement. Retrieved from https://socialwelfare.library.vcu.edu/people/wald-lillian/

Brooks, V. W. (1989). Always a system: The feminism of Lillian Wald. New York: Feminist Press at the City University of New York.

Feld, M. N. (2008). Lillian Wald: A biography. Chapel Hill: University of North Carolina Press.

Wald, L. D. (1915). The house on Henry Street. New York: Henry Holt and Company. New York Times. (1933, March 5). From Windows on the World. Retrieved from https://www.nytimes.com/1933/03/05/archives/from-windows-on-the-world.html

Emma Goldman

Goldman, E. (1931). Living My Life. Alfred A. Knopf. Connolly CA. "I am a trained nurse": the nursing identity of anarchist and radical

Emma Goldman. Nurs Hist Rev. 2010;18:84-99. doi: 10.1891/1062-8061.18.84. PMID: 20067092.

Goldman, E. (1910). Anarchism and Other Essays. Mother Earth Publishing Association.

Gornick, V. (2011). Emma Goldman: Revolution as a Way of Life. Yale University Press.

Connolly, C. (2020) Radicalization of a Nurse: The Story of Emma Goldman.

Adah Samuels Thoms

Alexander Street Press. (n.d.). Adah Belle Samuels Thoms: A biography. Retrieved from https://documents.alexanderstreet.com/d/1010597921 Thoms AB. Of Interest to Nurses. J Natl Med Assoc. 1919 Apr-Jun;11(2):86. PMCID:PMC2622075.

Thoms, A. B. (1929). A History in the Making. AJN The American Journal of Nursing, 29(5), 560.

Althea T. Davis, Early Black American Leaders in Nursing: Architects for Integration and Equality, Jones & Bartlett Publishers, 1999 (ISBN 0-7637-1009-1 (study of Mary Eliza Mahoney, Martha Minerva Franklin, and Adah Belle Samuels Thoms)

Smith DB. The racial integration of medical and nursing associations in the United States. Hosp Health Serv Adm. 1992 Fall;37(3):387-401. PMID: 10120497.

Threat, C. J. (2015). Nursing civil rights: Gender and race in the Army Nurse Corps. (Women, Gender, and Sexuality in American History). Urbana, IL: University of Illinois Press.

Thoms, A. B. (1929). Pathfinders: A history of the progress of colored graduate nurses. Kay Printing House. https://babel.hathitrust.org/cgi/pt?id=mdp.39015012320084&seq=2

Harriet Boyd Hawes

Allsebrook, M. (1992). Born to Rebel: The Life of Harriet Boyd Hawes. Oxbow Books.

Women in Archaeology. (2021, June 6). Harriet Boyd Hawes: Tale of Two Cities. Retrieved from https://womeninarchaeology.com/2021/06/06/harriet-boyd-hawes-tale-two-cities/

Smith College Special Collections. (n.d.). Harriet Boyd Hawes Papers. Retrieved from https://findingaids.smith.edu/repositories/4/resources/5

New Republic. (2023). Harriet Boyd and Cora Stewart Crane: War Correspondents in Greece. Retrieved from https://newrepublic.com/article/175166/harriet-boyd-cora-stewart-crane-war- correspondents-greece

New York Times. (1904, September 25). Woman Discovers a Buried City in Crete: Miss Harriet Boyd's Campaigns. Retrieved from https://www.nytimes.com/1904/09/25/archives/woman- discovers-a-buried-city-in-crete-miss-harriet-boyds-campaigns.html

Hawes, H. B., Williams, B. E., Seager, R. B., & Hall, E. H. (2014). Gournia, Vasiliki, and Other Prehistoric Sites on the Isthmus of Hierapetra, Crete: Excavations of the Wells-Houston-Cramp Expeditions 1901, 1903, 1904 (2nd ed.). INSTAP Academic Press.

Smith College. (2008, Spring). Smith College Relief Unit: The Daring Women of Smith College's Relief Unit. Retrieved from https://www.smith.edu/newssmith/spring2008/france.php

Mount Holyoke College. (n.d.). Harriet Boyd Hawes. Retrieved from https://commons.mtholyoke.edu/foundingsisters/harriet-boyd-hawes/

Willig, L. (2021). Band of Sisters. HarperCollins Publishers. Retrieved from https://laurenwillig.com/books/band-of-sisters/

Sophia Duleep Singh

Anand, A. (2015). Sophia: Princess, Revolutionary. Bloomsbury Publishing. Dalrymple, W., & Anand, A. (Hosts). (2022). Sophia Duleep Singh [Audio podcast episode]. In Empire. Goalhanger Podcasts. https://www.goalhangerpodcasts.com/empire

Historic Royal Palaces. (n.d.). Sophia Duleep Singh. Retrieved from https://www.hrp.org.uk/hampton-court-palace/history-and-stories/sophia-duleep- singh/#gs.idhuff

Suffrage Resources. (n.d.). Princess Sophia Duleep Singh. Retrieved from https://www.suffrageresources.org.uk/resource/3219/princess-sophia-duleep-singh

BBC News. (2023, July 17). India's princess Sophia Duleep Singh: The suffragette royal who fought for women's rights. Retrieved from https://www.bbc.com/news/world-asia-india- 66220501

Mukherjee, S. (2011). Herabai Tata and Sophia Duleep Singh: Suffragette Resistances for India and Britain, 1910–1920. In S. Mukherjee (Ed.), South Asian Resistances in Britain, 1858- 1947 (pp. 106). Continuum.

Mukherjee, S. (2015). Born for trouble. TLS. Times Literary Supplement, (5840), 13-14.

Elena Arizmendi Mejía

Texas State Historical Association. (n.d.). Arizmendi Mejía, Elena Irene. In Handbook of Texas Online. Retrieved December 12, 2024, from https://www.tshaonline.org/handbook/entries/arizmendi-mejia-elena-irene Cano, G. (2010). Se llamaba Elena Arizmendi. Tusquets Editores México Knight, A. (2016). The Mexican Revolution: A very short introduction. Oxford University Press.

Arizmendi, E. (1927). Vida incompleta. M. Danon y Cí The New York Times. (1924, March 2). New women of Mexico striving for equality. The New York Times. https://www.nytimes.com/sitemap/1924/03/02/

Nella Larsen

Hutchinson, G. (2006). In Search of Nella Larsen: A Biography of the Color Line. Harvard University Press.

Larsen, N. (1929). Passing. Alfred A. Knopf.

WTTW Chicago. (n.d.). The Novelist Nella Larsen's Life Between Worlds. Retrieved from https://interactive.wttw.com/playlist/2020/07/17/nella-larsen

Gates, H. L. (2019, September 10). Nella Larsen Wrestled with Race and Sexuality in the Harlem Renaissance. The New York Times. Retrieved from https://www.nytimes.com/interactive/2018/obituaries/overlooked-nella-larsen.html

Vera Brittain

Brittain, V. (2005). Testament of youth: An autobiographical study of the years 1900–1925. Penguin Books. (Original work published 1933)

Bostridge, M. (2014). Vera Brittain and the First World War: The story of Testament of youth. Bloomsbury Academic.

Fell, C. (2014). A feminist view of Vera Brittain's Testament of youth. Retrieved from https://www.gerflint.fr/Base/RU-Irlande4/fell.pdf

Williamson, G. (2013, August 21). Testament of youth: Vera Brittain's classic, 80 years on. The Guardian. Retrieved from https://www.theguardian.com/books/2013/mar/24/vera-brittain-testament-of-youth

Susie Walking Bear Yellowtail

Theobold, B. (2016). Nurse, Mother, Midwife: Susie Walking Bear Yellowtail and the Struggle for Crow Women's Reproductive Autonomy. Montana: The Magazine of Western History, 66(3), 17-35. https://www.niwrc.org/sites/default/files/images/resource/theobald-_nurse_mother_midwife_%20%281%29.pdf

Nursing Clio. (2020, November 19). Susie Walking Bear Yellowtail and Histories of Native American Nursing. Retrieved from https://nursingclio.org/2020/11/19/susie-walking-bear- yellowtail-and-histories-of-native-american-nursing/

Himmelfarb Library. (2021, November 17). Native American Heritage Month: Susie Walking Bear Yellowtail. Retrieved from https://blogs.gwu.edu/himmelfarb/2021/11/17/native-american-heritage-month-susie-walking-bear-yellowtail/

Hinkell, T. (2000). Nurse of the 20th Century: Susie Walking Bear Yellowtail: First Native American Registered Nurse. https://books.google.com/books/about/Nurse_of_the_20th_Century.html?id=d8FKGwAAC AAJ

Irena Sendler & Ala Golab-Grynburg

Mazzeo, T. J., & Carlin, A. (n.d.). Irena's Children: The Extraordinary Story of the Woman Who Saved 2,500 Children from the Warsaw Ghetto.

Mieszkowska, A., & Zbirohowski-Koscia, W. (2010, November 18). Irena Sendler: Mother of the Children of the Holocaust.

Margaret Charles Smith

Smith, M. C., & Holmes, L. J. (1996). Listen to Me Good: The Life Story of an Alabama Midwife. Ohio State University Press.

The New York Times. (2004, November 17). Margaret Charles Smith, 99, Midwife Who Delivered 3500 Babies.

Steckel, R. H. (n.d.). Fertility and Mortality in the United States. EH.Net. Retrieved from https://eh.net/encyclopedia/fertility-and-mortality-in-the-united-states/ Williamsons, E. (2014). "Miss Margaret – the story of an Alabama Granny Midwife." YouTube. https://youtu.be/XbCalkT7jrM?si=BVMcAS_TlUf-lDoD

Simone Weil

Collins, R. K. L. (2021). Parachute woman: Simone Weil's front-line nurses proposal. Epoché Magazine. Retrieved from https://epochemagazine.org/37/parachute-woman-simone-weils- front-line-nurses-proposal/

Popova, M. (n.d.). Simone Weil on temptation, the key to discipline, and how to be a complete human being. The Marginalian. Retrieved from https://www.themarginalian.org

du Plessix Gray, F. (2001). Simone Weil. Viking Press. Weil, S. (1951). Waiting for God (E. Craufurd, Trans.). Harper & Row

Springsted, E. O. (Ed.). (1998). Simone Weil: Essential writings. Orbis Books.

Ruth Davidow

Ehrlich, R., & Ehrlich, H. J. (2002). In the Shadow of Power: American Institutions of Empire. Rutgers University Press.

Graham, H. (2005). The Spanish Civil War: A Very Short Introduction. Oxford University Press. Retrieved from

D'Antonio, P. (Ed.). (2002). Nursing History Review. Springer Publishing Company.

Gold, M. (2018, August 10). Meet the radical nurse who joined the Spanish Civil War. Forward. Retrieved from https://forward.com/culture/407978/meet-the-radical-nurse-who-joined-the- spanish-civil-war/

Associated Press. (2001, October 4). Ruth Davidow. SFGATE. Retrieved from https://www.sfgate.com/news/article/Ruth-Davidow-2919968.php

Canby, V. (1984, March 28). Screen: Good Fight, Spanish war. The New York Times. Retrieved from https://www.nytimes.com/1984/03/28/movies/screen-good-fight-spanish-war.html Ruth

Davidow papers, 1975–1998. Rare Book & Manuscript Library, University of Illinois at Urbana-Champaign.

YouTube. (n.d.). Good Fight, Ruth Davidow segment. [Video]. YouTube. Retrieved November 24, 2024, from https://youtu.be/f_G_JkaTlBU?si=DCDl3Fis7LEdK2Py

Salaria Kea O'Reilly

Johnson, A. (2007). Healing the wounds of fascism: The American Medical Brigade and the Spanish Civil War (Master's thesis).

Moruno, D. M. (n.d.). Salaria Kea's memories from the Spanish Civil War. Academia.edu. https://www.academia.edu/29594831/Salaria_Keas_memories_from_the_Spanish_civil_war_pdf

Kea, S. (1938). A Negro nurse in Spain. New York: The Negro Committee to Aid Spain.

Martin, F. (1936–1988). Fredericka Martin papers. Series I: Medical personnel: Biographical files and correspondence. (Pamphlet: "A Negro Nurse in Republican Spain" reprint of 1938 publication).

O'Reilly, S. K. (1980, June 7). Salaria Kea O'Reilly interview. In J. Gerassi (Interviewer), John Gerassi oral history collection. ALBA.AUDIO.018. Box 1, Folders 18-152 to 18-153. Tamiment Library/Robert F. Wagner Labor Archives, New York University.

BlackPast. (n.d.). Salaria Kea O'Reilly (1913– 1991). BlackPast.org. https://www.blackpast.org/african-american-history/reilly-salaria-kee-1913-1991

Abraham Lincoln Brigade Archives. (n.d.). Salaria Kea: A Negro nurse in Republican Spain. ALBA. https://alba-valb.org/resource/salaria-kea-a-negro-nurse-in-republican-spain/

Patai, D. (1993). Heroines of the good fight: Testimonies of U.S. volunteer nurses in the Spanish Civil War, 1936–1939. Nursing History Review: Official Journal of the American Association for the History of Nursing, 1(1), 97–114.

Albertina Sisulu

History.com Editors. (n.d.). Apartheid. HISTORY. https://www.history.com/topics/africa/apartheid

Tolsma, M. & Downing, C. (2016). An integrative review of Albertina Sisulu and ubuntu : relevance to caring and nursing. Health SA Gesondheid, 21(1), 176– 185. https://journals.co.za/doi/abs/10.1016/j.hsag.2016.04.002

Sisulu, E. (2002). Walter and Albertina Sisulu: In our lifetime. David Philip Publishers.

 Earl G. Albertina Sisulu 1918-2011 Nurse and South African anti-apartheid activist.Nursing Standard (Royal College of Nursing (Great Britain) : 1987). 2011 Jul;25(45):33. DOI: 10.7748/ns.25.45.33.s46. PMID: 28086716. https://europepmc.org/article/med/28086716

Mandela, N. (1994). Long walk to freedom: the autobiography of Nelson Mandela. Boston, Little, Brown

Marie Branch

Branch, M. (1974). Faculty development to meet minority group needs: Recruitment, retention, and curriculum change, 1971-74. Final report. ERIC. https://files.eric.ed.gov/fulltext/ED123982.pdf

Branch, M. (1977). Providing safe nursing care for ethnic people of color. Nurse Educator, 2(4), 6– 8. https://journals.lww.com/nurseeducatoronline/Citation/1977/07000/Providing_Safe_Nursing _Care_for_Ethnic_People_of.6.aspx Library of Congress. (n.d.). Interview with Mildred Pitts Walters. Library of Congress. https://www.loc.gov/item/2015669158/

Nelson, A. (2011). Body and soul: The Black Panther Party and the fight against discrimination. University of Minnesota Press.

Gatrall, C.E. (2020, October 29). Marie Branch and the power of nursing. Nursing Clio.https://nursingclio.org/2020/10/29/marie-branch-and-the-power-of-nursing/

Shirley Willer

Marcus, E. (Host). (1990). Shirley Willer [Audio podcast episode]. In Making Gay History. Making Gay History. Retrieved from https://makinggayhistory.com/podcast/episode-12-shirley-willer/

Willer, S. (1992). One angry nurse. In E. Marcus (Ed.), Making history: The struggle for gay and lesbian equal rights, 1945–1990: An oral history. HarperCollins.

www.ingramcontent.com/pod-product-compliance
Lightning Source LLC
Chambersburg PA
CBHW051314120626
46547CB00015B/2237